Contents

TABLES

FIGURES

ANTHROPOLOGICAL PAPERS OF
THE UNIVERSITY OF ARIZONA
NUMBER 82

Households on the Mimbres Horizon

Excavations at La Gila Encantada, Southwestern New Mexico

Barbara J. Roth

WITH CONTRIBUTIONS BY

Christina Dykstra

Jeffrey R. Ferguson

Linda M. Gregonis

Thomas E. Gruber

Pamela J. McBride

Dylan J. Person

Bruce G. Phillips

Danielle Romero

Denise Ruzicka

Kari Schmidt Cates

Mollie S. Toll

Arthur W. Vokes

THE UNIVERSITY OF
ARIZONA PRESS

TUCSON

The University of Arizona Press
www.uapress.arizona.edu

Printed in the United States of America.

28 27 26 25 24 23   6 5 4 3 2 1

ISBN-13: 978-0-8165-4854-5 (paper)
          978-0-8165-4855-2 (ebook)

Editing and indexing by Linda Gregonis.
InDesign layout by Douglas Goewey.

Library of Congress Cataloging-in-Publication Data
Names: Roth, Barbara J., 1958– author.
Title: Households on the Mimbres horizon : excavations
    at La Gila Encantada, southwestern New Mexico /
    Barbara J. Roth ; with contributions by: Christina
    Dykstra [and eleven others].
Other titles: Excavations at La Gila Encantada,
    southwestern New Mexico | Anthropological papers of
    the University of Arizona ; no. 82.
Description: [Tucson] : The University of Arizona Press,
    2023. | Series: Anthropological papers of the University
    of Arizona ; number 82 | Includes bibliographical
    references.
Identifiers: LCCN 2022026736 (print) | LCCN 2022026737
    (ebook) | ISBN 9780816548545 (paperback)
    | ISBN 9780816548552 (ebook)
Subjects: LCSH: Mimbres culture—New Mexico—Grant
    County. | Pit houses—New Mexico—Grant County.
    | Earthworks (Archaeology)—New Mexico—Grant
    County. | Excavations (Archaeology)—New Mexico—
    Grant County. | La Gila Encantada Site (N.M.) | Grant
    County (N.M.)—Antiquities.
Classification: LCC E99.M76 (print) | LCC E99.M76
    (ebook) | DDC 978.9/01—dc23/eng/20221014
LC record available at https://lccn.loc.gov/2022026736
LC ebook record available at https://lccn.loc.gov/
    2022026737

Cover Photos: Overview of La Gila Encantada, looking south towards Silver City. The lozenge-shaped artifact on the left, found in Pithouse 2, was made from a Mimbres Black-on-white Style 1 sherd; the mano and metate at lower right, found in Pithouse 8, were used by a left-handed person. Photos by Danielle Romero (overview and pottery artifact) and Barbara Roth (metate and mano).

ABOUT THE AUTHOR

BARBARA J. ROTH is a professor in the Department of Anthropology at the University of Nevada, Las Vegas (UNLV). Her research focuses on the Mimbres region of southwestern New Mexico, where she has excavated several pithouse sites and more recently directed excavations at Elk Ridge, a Classic period pueblo. She received her Ph.D. in anthropology from the University of Arizona.

ABOUT THE CONTRIBUTORS

CHRISTINA DYKSTRA received her undergraduate degree from the Department of Anthropology at the University of Nevada, Las Vegas.

JEFFREY R. FERGUSON is a research associate professor at the Archaeometry Laboratory at MURR in Columbia, Missouri, and an assistant professor in the Department of Anthropology at the University of Missouri. He received his Ph.D. in anthropology from the University of Colorado.

LINDA M. GREGONIS is an independent archaeological researcher in Tucson, specializing in ceramic analysis. She has a master's degree in anthropology from the University of Arizona. Linda is currently the editor of the Anthropological Papers of the University of Arizona.

THOMAS E. GRUBER is owner of Open Range Archaeology, LLC, a private Cultural Resource Management firm in Norman, Oklahoma. He received his Ph.D. in anthropology from the University of Oklahoma.

PAMELA J. MCBRIDE is a paleoethnobotanist in the Paleoethnobotany Laboratory in the Office of Archaeological Studies at the Museum of New Mexico, Albuquerque.

DYLAN J. PERSON is a Ph.D. candidate in the Department of Anthropology at the University of Nevada, Las Vegas, specializing in the study of lithic technology in the Mimbres region.

BRUCE G. PHILLIPS is owner of BGP Consulting in Flagstaff, Arizona, which provides geoarchaeological and ethnobotanical services to archaeological firms and researchers.

DANIELLE ROMERO is the director of the Western New Mexico University Museum in Silver City, New Mexico, and a Ph.D. candidate in the Department of Anthropology at the University of Nevada, Las Vegas. She specializes in the study of ceramics from pithouse and pueblo sites in the Mimbres region.

DENISE RUZICKA received her master's degree in anthropology from the University of Nevada, Las Vegas. She currently works for the California Department of Forestry and Fire Prevention.

KARI SCHMIDT CATES is a senior staff scientist with Environmental Planning Group in Tempe, Arizona. She received her Ph.D. in anthropology from the University of New Mexico.

MOLLIE S. TOLL is a paleoethnobotanist in the Paleoethnobotany Lab at the Office of Archaeological Studies, Museum of New Mexico, Albuquerque.

ARTHUR W. VOKES has a master's degree in anthropology from the University of Arizona. He was the Curator and Manager of the Archaeological Repository Collections at the Arizona State Museum for 30 years before retiring in 2020. He has specialized in research on shell artifacts.

Acknowledgments

I would like to take this opportunity to thank some of the many people who made this project possible. Thanks are due to the Archaeological Conservancy, specifically to Jim Walker, for granting permission to do the work at the site; to Bob Schiowitz, who first told me about La Gila Encantada and convinced me that it would be a great place to work; and to Dr. Dennis McMullen for granting permission to work on two pithouses located on land that he owns on the west side of the site.

Many people participated in the excavations at La Gila Encantada (Appendix) and thanks are due to each one of them, especially the late Leon Lorentzen, who served as the field director and my sounding board; Robert "Jake" Hickerson, crew chief for both excavation seasons; the late Jodi Dalton, crew chief in 2004; and Beau Schriever, lab director. Hearty thanks to the Grant County Archaeological Society volunteers and other volunteers who helped us dig, screen, and backfill, without whom we literally could not have finished the project (Appendix). Special thanks are due to Marilyn Markel, Judy and Carroll Welch, Josh Reeves, Kyle Meredith, and Carol McCanless (Russell). Nancy Curtis made this project possible by letting us use her water, park in her driveway, and generally disrupt her life for six weeks every summer. The inferences made in this report have come from years of discussion with Roger Anyon, Darrell Creel, Pat Gilman, Danielle Romero, and Bob Stokes. I thank them for their input, insights, and support.

CHAPTER ONE

Introduction: Households on the Mimbres Horizon

Pithouse sites represent the basic form of settlement in the Mimbres Mogollon region of southwestern New Mexico for much of the prehistoric occupation, spanning the period from A.D. 200 to the late 900s. Yet despite its predominance in terms of the time sequence (Anyon and others 2017), the Pithouse period has often been viewed as a way station on the way to the Classic Mimbres period (A.D. 1000–1130), best known for its elaborate black-on-white pottery and cobble adobe pueblos. Pithouse sites played an important role in the initial classification of the Mimbres branch of the Mogollon (Haury 1936; Wheat 1955). These early investigations of pithouse components beneath pueblos and of pithouse sites themselves generally focused on architecture and ceramics, which were used to classify them and document the development of the Mimbres Mogollon through time. As a result, only limited attention has been paid to the variability in pithouse occupations across the Mimbres area, with most researchers focusing instead on shared material culture and the distinctiveness of the Mimbres in relation to other southwestern cultural groups.

This monograph seeks to explore some of the variability present in pithouse occupations in the Mimbres region using the La Gila Encantada site (LA 113467) as a case study. The goal of this study is to show that the variability present in pithouse occupations across time and space was tied to multiple factors including environmental differences, economic practices, and the social composition of groups occupying the sites. The Pithouse period was not static and homogeneous but instead exhibited variation that can be used to explore issues related to differences in diet, sedentism, and social organization.

La Gila Encantada is an upland site situated away from the Mimbres and Gila river valleys. Its residents do not appear to have been involved in the economic and social networks that were participated in by people living in riverine settings. Yet, the site exhibits many of the characteristics generally used to classify Mimbres Pithouse period occupations and at some level its inhabitants participated in region-wide social dynamics (Anyon and Roth 2018; Haury 1936). Investigations at La Gila Encantada thus provide supplemental data to studies of larger riverine pithouse sites (Anyon and LeBlanc 1984; Creel 2006; Roth 2015; Sedig 2015; Shafer 2003) and establish a framework for addressing why differences in these occupations developed and how those differences impacted the overall cultural trajectories in the Mimbres region.

The research goals addressed during this project focused on placing the households at La Gila Encantada into a broader context within the Mimbres region and using data recovered from the site to address how and why different household configurations developed. Despite basic similarities in overall adaptations, especially in terms of the environmental setting and access to agricultural technology and knowledge, some Late Pithouse period groups went on very different trajectories than others. Swanson, Anyon, and Nelson (2012) link much of this to agricultural potential, arguing that during the Late Pithouse period sites located in areas with high agricultural potential in terms of access to arable land and reliable water supplies represent larger populations with longer occupations. This clearly seems to be the case at sites along the river terraces in the Mimbres River Valley (Galaz, NAN, Old Town, Harris) and probably the Gila River Valley (Sedig 2015), although less is known about the nature of the Late Pithouse period occupations there. Yet the large agricultural villages with evidence of some level of social complexity only portray part of the picture of Late Pithouse period adaptations. Smaller sites dot the landscape and their inhabitants participated in regional dynamics in varying ways (Swanson, Anyon, and Nelson 2012).

Fieldwork at La Gila Encantada provided an opportunity to examine one of these smaller sites and address issues of concern to archaeologists in the U.S. Southwest and those studying Neolithic societies elsewhere. La Gila Encantada represents what by today's standards would be considered a rural occupation, yet it shares some basic architectural and artifact traits with other contemporary sites throughout the region. Excavations at La Gila Encantada thus provided insights into the economic and social relationships involved in living in a small pithouse village away from, but possibly still connected to, the larger villages. This monograph explores the daily lives of people who lived at La Gila Encantada by addressing their household activities, subsistence practices, and the nature of social interaction with other groups. As such, it provides a window into lesser-known small-scale occupations that were present worldwide after the transition to agriculture.

THE PITHOUSE PERIOD IN THE MIMBRES REGION

Current models of the Pithouse period have been informed primarily by work done in the major river valleys, especially the Mimbres River Valley (Figure 1.1; Anyon 1980; Anyon and LeBlanc 1984; Anyon and Roth 2018; Diehl and LeBlanc 2001; Roth 2015; Roth and Baustian 2015; Shafer 2003; Swanson, Anyon, and Nelson 2012). Earlier excavations by Emil Haury (1936) at the Harris site and Mogollon Village in the 1930s established the general sequence of the Pithouse period based primarily on changes in architecture and ceramics. For the most part, this sequence is still used today (Table 1.1; see also Anyon and others 2017 for a recent update on the chronology).

The Early Pithouse period (A.D. 200–550) is characterized by the initial use of brownware ceramics (Alma Plain) and the construction of circular pithouses (Anyon, Gilman, and LeBlanc 1981; Diehl and LeBlanc 2001). Early Pithouse period sites in the Mimbres region are generally located on ridgetops, most likely for monitoring seasonally available resources (Diehl 2001). Most researchers see the Early Pithouse period as representing a mixed farming-foraging subsistence strategy, with groups moving seasonally and most likely over-wintering at pithouse sites. Survey work by Patricia Gilman in the Deming region south of the Mimbres River Valley has identified seasonal camps that were part of this mobile settlement-subsistence strategy.

No Early Pithouse period occupation was identified at La Gila Encantada.

The Late Pithouse period is divided into three phases based on ceramic and architectural changes: the Georgetown, San Francisco, and Three Circle phases. The Georgetown phase (A.D. 550–650) in the Mimbres region is characterized by generally small sites with round or D-shaped pithouses and plainware (Alma Plain) and redware ceramics. In the Mimbres River Valley, Georgetown phase sites are located on terraces next to the river, leading researchers to argue that this phase was associated with growing dependence on agriculture (Anyon 1980; Anyon and LeBlanc 1984). The first communal structures were present at Georgetown phase sites in the Mimbres Valley. They consisted of round structures that were larger than domestic structures and had distinct adobe lobes near their entryways (Anyon and LeBlanc 1980). Few subsistence remains have been recovered from Georgetown phase sites, but groups apparently focused primarily on hunting and gathering, with maize agriculture used as a supplement. It is possible that stored maize allowed an over-wintering strategy that led to seasonal sedentism.

The San Francisco phase (A.D. 650–750) is characterized by square pithouses with rounded corners, ramp entryways, and the first production of decorated ceramics, Mogollon Red-on-brown. Communal structures were round but substantially larger than domestic structures by this period. Subsistence remains indicate an increasing focus on maize agriculture, although wild foods still comprised an important component of the diet. During the San Francisco phase, major developments in community growth began. At the Harris site in the Mimbres River Valley, Roth and Baustian (2015) have documented the initial presence of extended family corporate groups that they argue developed as a result of labor needs associated with agricultural intensification.

During the Three Circle phase (A.D. 750–1000), substantial changes occurred in Mimbres pithouse communities, especially in the Mimbres and Gila river valleys. Many researchers tie these changes to a growing dependence on agriculture, possibly including an increased focus on irrigation (Anyon and Roth 2018; Creel 2006; Roth and Baustian 2015; Shafer 2003, 2006). Large pithouse villages are present along the Mimbres River at Harris (Haury 1936; Roth 2015), Old Town (Creel 2006), NAN Ranch (Shafer 2003), Swarts (Cosgrove and Cosgrove 1932), and Galaz (Anyon and LeBlanc 1984); and along the Gila River at Lee Village (Bussey 1975) and the Woodrow site (Sedig 2015). Pithouses were rectangular with ramp entryways

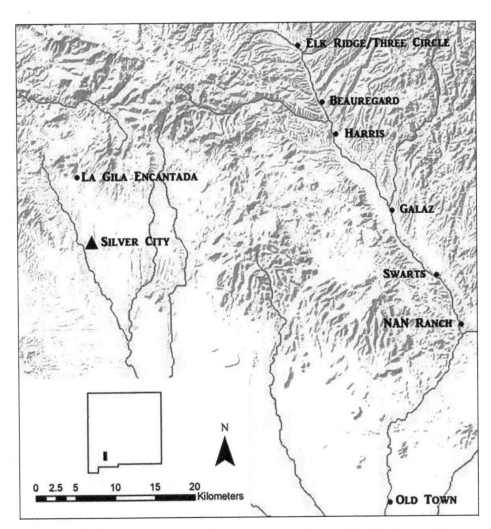

Figure 1.1. Pithouse sites in the Mimbres Valley in relation to La Gila Encantada, which is west of the Mimbres Valley near Silver City, New Mexico. Other sites shown here include (from south to north) Old Town, NAN Ranch Ruin, Swarts, Galaz, Harris, Beauregard, and Three Circle/Elk Ridge. Map by Danielle Romero.

Table 1.1. Mimbres Mogollon Cultural Sequence

Period and Phase	Dates	Ceramic Types and Styles	House Form
Early Pithouse Period	AD 200–550	Alma Plain	Circular pithouse
Late Pithouse Period			
Georgetown Phase	AD 550–650	Alma Plain San Francisco Red	Circular or D-shaped pithouse with ramp entry
San Francisco Phase	AD 650–750	Mogollon Red-on-brown	Rectangular pithouse with rounded corners
Three Circle Phase	AD 750–1000	Three Circle Red-on-white Mimbres Black-on-white Style I (Boldface) Mimbres Black-on-white Style II (Mangas)	Rectangular pithouse
Classic Period	AD 1000–1130	Mimbres Black-on-white Style III (Classic) Mimbres Polychrome	Cobble adobe pueblos

Data for table derived from Diehl: 1996:104; Anyon, Gilman, and LeBlanc 1981; Anyon et al. 2017.

and often exhibit evidence of remodeling or replastering. Ceramic technology also changed during the Three Circle phase. Three Circle Red-on-white was produced by the mid-A.D. 700s, followed quickly by a shift to Mimbres Black-on-white Style I (Boldface) ceramics. Changes in site layout have been documented during this period, with evidence from the Harris site (Roth and Baustian 2015; Roth 2019b), Old Town (Creel 2006; Lucas 2007), and NAN Ranch (Shafer 2003) indicating the presence of extended family corporate groups. This shift in site organization was accompanied by the construction of large, rectangular great kivas at the larger villages. Many of them opened onto central plazas containing burials and cremations (Shafer 2003; Creel and Shafer 2015). The largest structures at the largest villages were ritually retired by burning toward the end of the Three Circle phase (Creel and Anyon 2003; Creel, Anyon, and Roth 2015).

As is apparent from this brief overview, information on the Late Pithouse period in this area comes primarily from work done in the Mimbres River Valley, generally from large sites. As a result, many interpretations of Pithouse period occupations have focused on river-based adaptations. Little work has been done away from the river valleys, so our understanding of the nature of pithouse occupations in these areas is limited. Work at La Gila Encantada was done expressly to increase our knowledge of Late Pithouse period occupations away from the river and to explore the variability present in Late Pithouse period pithouse occupations across the Mimbres region.

RESEARCH GOALS

Research at La Gila Encantada was done to determine whether smaller, nonriverine Late Pithouse period occupations exhibited different trajectories than those seen in the lowland river valleys and, if so, what accounted for these differences. This study builds on the author's previous work at the Lake Roberts Vista site (LA 71877), located on a ridge top above Sapillo Creek in the Sapillo Valley, a tributary of the Gila River (Roth 2007). Work at Lake Roberts showed that groups initially moved seasonally into the Sapillo Valley during the Georgetown phase to hunt large game such as deer, gather piñon nuts, and farm. This seasonal use apparently continued until the Three Circle phase, when groups became more sedentary and more dependent on agriculture. This relatively rapid shift to sedentism and agricultural dependence contrasts with evidence from

the Mimbres River Valley, where sedentism, agricultural intensification, and associated social changes occurred by the San Francisco phase and continued through the Three Circle phase.

Lake Roberts appeared to represent a different trajectory of social and economic change than that observed in the Mimbres River Valley (Roth 2007). However, because the pithouse component was beneath a heavily looted pueblo, it was not possible to fully evaluate the nature and causes of the observed differences and it was also not clear if Lake Roberts was unique or representative of a broader pattern of pithouse occupations away from the river. La Gila Encantada did not have a pueblo component on it (except for a possible small field house at the southern end of the site) so it was possible to more fully evaluate the nature of the pithouse occupation and to address whether it represents this different kind of cultural configuration. This was accomplished by addressing three main research topics: mobility strategies, subsistence practices, and household organization.

Mobility Strategies

As noted previously, current data from sites in the Mimbres River Valley support the Mimbres Foundation's idea of a linear trajectory of increased sedentism and agricultural dependence with full sedentary, agriculturally dependent groups present by A.D. 800 at the latest, and possibly earlier during the San Francisco phase (Anyon, Gilman, and LeBlanc 1981; Anyon and LeBlanc 1984). Based on Stokes' (1995) survey of the Sapillo Valley and fieldwork at the Lake Roberts Vista Site, Stokes and Roth (1999) proposed that in contrast, groups in the Sapillo Valley remained relatively mobile late into the Pithouse period. The transition to sedentism appears to have occurred rapidly during the Three Circle phase in the Sapillo. This may have been the case for other upland valleys in the Mimbres region, but the lack of investigations at sites away from the river made this difficult to assess. Excavations at La Gila Encantada were done to gain additional insights into the timing and nature of the shift to sedentism in another area outside the Mimbres River Valley.

Although consistently debated, most researchers agree that sedentism is associated with particular aspects of architecture, site structure, and material culture (Kelly 1992; Rafferty 1985). These include formal architecture, storage, burials, and dense trash deposits. Diehl and Gilman (1996) and Lightfoot (1984) spell out the architectural changes associated with increased sedentism in the

Mogollon region including the presence of formal hearths, plastered walls and floors, more durable wall construction, and evidence of remodeling. Sedentism is also highly correlated with storage (Keeley 1988; Kent 1992). The presence of large storage pits in communal use areas at the Harris site is one of the main indicators of both sedentism and the important role of extended family corporate groups (Roth 2019b), but these have not been found regularly at other Pithouse period sites, in large part because of the lack of excavation in extramural areas. Excavations at La Gila Encantada were geared toward locating extramural features associated with houses, which would include storage features.

Several other lines of evidence were used to address this topic, including structural remains and construction techniques, artifact diversity and distribution, and the presence of botanical and faunal seasonal markers. These data provide a comparative framework when combined with data from other upland and riverine sites.

Subsistence Practices

The second topic, the degree of agricultural dependence of Pithouse period groups, is one that has been the most consistently addressed for the Pithouse period. Diehl (1996) used paleobotanical data to argue that the introduction of a new strain of eight-rowed maize around A.D. 700 led to increased agricultural dependence in the Mogollon region, providing larger yields that were easier to grind than earlier varieties. The new maize variety was apparently correlated with an increase in the use of trough metates, which Adams (1999) has shown are more efficient for grinding maize. Overall, with the exception of Diehl's inclusion of paleobotanical data, however, most studies of Pithouse period subsistence have focused on indirect evidence of subsistence (e.g., mano size; Hard 1990). At La Gila Encantada, multiple lines of evidence including paleobotanical, pollen, faunal, and ground stone data were used to reconstruct subsistence strategies.

At the beginning of the Late Pithouse period in the Mimbres River Valley, site locations shifted from high elevation points to lower elevations along terraces in the river valleys. This has been inferred to be tied to increased agricultural dependence (Anyon 1980). This change in site location is not apparent at La Gila Encantada nor at many other Late Pithouse period sites in tributary valleys. It is possible that groups in these settings were less dependent on agriculture than groups in the Mimbres Valley or in other upland valleys. Data from La Gila Encantada were used to evaluate these differences and determine if groups in upland settings remained less dependent on agriculture.

Household Organization

The third research topic involved examining household organization during the Late Pithouse period. A specific goal of this research was to determine if discrete households could be identified archaeologically. For this project, a household was defined following Kramer (1982:673) and Blanton (1994:5) as a group occupying a bounded residential space that shared domestic activities and decision making (see also Netting, Wilk, and Arnould 1984). Archaeologists in the U.S. Southwest generally use architecture as a basis for defining households (e.g., Lowell 1991), but artifact types and distributions can also be used to address the role of households within prehistoric societies (see Douglass and Gonlin 2012; Ciolek-Torrello 1985; Seymour 1990; Stokes 2019). The identification of households via the analysis of site structure, ceramics, absolute dates, pithouse floor assemblages, and extramural features was used to provide evidence of how groups were organized.

Households are distinguished by a set of social behaviors including the pooling and sharing of resources, food processing, cooking, eating, and manufacturing (Wilk and Rathje 1982; Rice 2003; Netting, Wilk, and Arnould 1984). These behaviors can be observed archaeologically by looking at the spatial distribution of material remains within architectural space. Artifact assemblages recovered from excavated houses and extramural features were used to examine household activities. This is a major contribution of this project, as most other excavation projects in this area have focused almost exclusively on structure excavations, in large part because the presence of pueblo components have prohibited the identification of associated extramural features.

The recovery of information on households at this site, when coupled with data from Lake Roberts Vista and compared with data from excavated sites along the Mimbres River Valley, allows for making further inferences concerning the social organization of Pithouse period groups. The author's work at the Harris site (Roth 2019b) documented three levels of site organization: (1) autonomous households, (2) pithouse clusters that are inferred to be the remains of extended family corporate groups, and (3) the Harris community, representing the integration of extended family and autonomous households via participation in communal rituals held in great kivas and a central plaza. The nature of households at La Gila Encantada appear to be substantially different than at riverine sites (Roth 2019a). The reasons for this disparity became a key topic of investigation as research at the site progressed. Household-related data provide important insights on the nature of and reasons for the development of differences in household and community organization between upland and riverine settings.

MONOGRAPH ORGANIZATION

The following chapters present data from excavations at La Gila Encantada that address the research questions described here. Chapter 2 discusses the fieldwork including field and analysis methods and excavation results of both pithouse and extramuraul features. Chapter 3 presents the ceramic data and how they relate to site chronology, household activities, and social interaction. This chapter includes a discussion of decorated, brown ware, red ware, and corrugated sherds, whole and reconstructible vessels, and worked sherds. Chapter 4 provides data on the chipped and ground stone recovered during excavations that were used to address mobility strategies and subsistence practices. Chapter 5 describes the shell, minerals and stone and bone jewelry from the site. Flotation, pollen, and faunal analysis results and their relation to subsistence practices are presented in Chapter 6. Chapter 7 summarizes the results of excavations at La Gila Encantada in light of the research questions.

CHAPTER TWO

Excavations at La Gila Encantada

The La Gila Encantada site is located in Little Walnut Canyon north of Silver City, New Mexico, on land owned by the Archaeological Conservancy (Figure 1.1). The site is above Little Walnut Creek in an open juniper woodland dominated by piñon pine and alligator-bark juniper in the Great Basin Conifer Woodland biotic community (Figure 2.1). The site location was optimal for several reasons: it provided access to multiple resource zones, including riparian resources (cattails, oak, walnut) along the creek and piñon-juniper on the hill slopes. Game is currently plentiful in the area despite rapid development and it was likely even more plentiful in the past. The ridge top provides a good view of a large expanse of floodplain at the base of the ridge, which would have been well-suited for agricultural fields. The inhabitants chose the only flat-topped area along this ridge line on which to build. Additional flat-topped ridges are visible south and east of the site and would have been similarly suited for Pithouse period occupations. No systematic survey has been done in Little Walnut Canyon, so it is not clear if La Gila Encantada is unique or part of a more widespread adaptation to nonriverine settings.

Fieldwork at La Gila Encantada involved surface collections, a magnetometer survey, and two seasons of excavations during which seven pithouses and nine extramural features were excavated (Roth 2010a). The site was originally recorded by archaeologists Powys Gadd and Bob Schiowitz from the Gila National Forest. They recorded a dense scatter of ceramics, lithics, and ground stone and mapped more than 20 surface depressions that they thought were pithouses. Test excavations were done at the site by archaeologists Ray Mauldin, Jeff Leach, and Fred Almarez in 1998. Their work involved mapping and some

limited excavations of several pithouses including a trench through Pithouse 22 and cleaning out a previously looted pithouse (Pithouse 23) that likely dated to the San Francisco phase. No report is available on that fieldwork, but Pithouse 22 was fully excavated during the current project.

Preliminary fieldwork was done at the site by the author, along with student and Grant County Archaeological Society volunteers, in the summer of 2003. As discussed in Chapter 1, this work was done as part of the author's research on Pithouse period occupations away from the Mimbres River Valley. Previous work at the Lake Roberts Vista site indicated that groups away from the river remained mobile for longer periods than those in the river valley, with a relatively rapid shift to sedentism during the Three Circle phase that was inferred to be tied to an increased dependence on agriculture (Roth 2007; Stokes and Roth 1999). La Gila Encantada represented an ideal location to examine whether this shift occurred in other nonriverine settings, because it represented a Pithouse period site away from the river that lacked a pueblo component, providing the possibility to examine change through time during the Pithouse period without disturbance by later pueblo building.

Preliminary work at the site involved mapping with a total station (EDM with laser theodolite), systematic surface collections, and in-field analysis. A 10-m by 10-m grid was placed over the major artifact concentration and 27 grid squares were collected and analyzed in the field (Roth 2004). One thousand thirty-three sherds were analyzed; the majority (85%) were Alma Plain (a plainware). Decorated wares were dominated by Mimbres Black-on-white Style I (Boldface) and Three Circle Red-on-white dating to the Three Circle phase; numerous indeterminate black-on-white ceramics were also recovered. These indicate

Figure 2.1. Photo of La Gila Encantada excavations looking south toward Silver City. Photo by Barbara Roth.

that the site dated primarily to the Three Circle phase, although six Mogollon Red-on-brown ceramics were also found, suggesting the potential for an earlier, San Francisco phase occupation.

Twenty-eight surface depressions representing possible pithouses were identified during this initial work. Based on a subsequent magnetometer survey and excavations, it appears that 19 of the identified surface depressions were pithouses; it is also likely that additional buried pithouses are present at the site. A small cobble pile at the southern end of the site (Feature 15) was thought to be a possible Classic period Mimbres field house when the site was initially recorded by the Forest Service, but no other architectural evidence of a pueblo period occupation was found and very few Mimbres Black-on-white Style III (Classic Mimbres) ceramics were recovered at the site.

Given the ceramic dating, location, and lack of a pueblo component at the site, a research proposal was submitted

to the Archaeological Conservancy to conduct excavations of a sample of pithouses to examine the research questions outlined in Chapter 1. Permission was obtained and additional fieldwork began in 2004. Prior to beginning excavations, a cesium magnetometer survey was done in the northwest portion of the site by Dr. Michael Rogers and his students from the Department of Physics at Ithaca College (Rogers and others 2010). The results revealed 11 possible pithouse locations. Subsequent excavations within three of these areas confirmed them as pithouses (Rogers and others 2010).

EXCAVATION METHODS

Pithouse Excavations

Pithouses dating to all three phases of the Late Pithouse period were excavated or tested during fieldwork at the site in 2004 and 2005 (Table 2.1; Figure 2.2). These excavations

Table 2.1. Excavated Pithouses at La Gila Encantada by Phase

Pithouse	Occupation Phase	Excavation Extent	Dates
14	Georgetown	Fully excavated	600-660 (I=640)[c]
			380-530 (I=420)[c]
22	San Francisco	Fully excavated	670-690 (I = 660)[c],
			679v[d]
23	San Francisco[a]	Previously excavated	
2	Three Circle	Fully excavated	735-865[b] (wall)
			660-710 (I = 680)[c]
			790-900 (I = 880)[c]
8	Three Circle (early)	¾ excavated	690-810 (I = 770)[c]
9	Three Circle	Tested: 1-m × 3-m unit	835-1015[b] (hearth)
			810-840; 860-910, 920-960 (I=890)[c]
20	Three Circle	Tested: 4-m × 2-m unit	
25	Three Circle	Tested: 4-m × 2-m unit	770-900 (I = 810, 840, 860)[c]

Key:
a. Previously tested by Raymond Mauldin.
b. Archaeomagnetic dates determined using Sternberg's (1982) statistical dating method.
c. One sigma, calibrated date; all radiocarbon dates were calibrated using INTCAL 98 (Stuiver, Reimer, and Braziunas 1998).
d. Dendrochronological date.
I = intercept point.
v = near cutting date.

were done as field schools from the University of Nevada, Las Vegas, directed by the author with help from volunteers from the Grant Country Archaeological Society (see Appendix for a list of participants). The pithouses were numbered following the system used by the Forest Service when the site was originally recorded.

The pithouses were excavated using a series of contiguous 2-m by 2-m units, with the exception of Pithouse 9, which was tested with one 1-m by 3-m unit. All pithouse fill was excavated in 10-cm levels and screened through ¼-inch mesh screen. Once roof fall/wall fall was encountered, it was excavated as a natural level, as were the floor fill and the floor. Sediments from the floor and floor fill were screened through ⅛-inch mesh screen. Once the pithouse excavations were completed, the pithouses and internal features were mapped using a total station.

Flotation and pollen samples were taken from trash fill, all features, and floor contexts. Radiocarbon and dendrochronology samples were taken from structural wood found in the roof fall or on the floor and from floor features. Archaeomagnetic samples were taken from the hearths of Pithouses 2, 9, and 14, and from the wall plaster of Pithouses 2 and 14. All flotation, pollen, faunal, and dating samples were sent to specialists for analysis. Samples were chosen for analysis based on their contexts

and potential to aid in addressing the research questions. Flotation analysis was done by Pamela McBride and Mollie Toll of the Office of Archaeological Studies, Museum of New Mexico, in Santa Fe; pollen samples were analyzed by Bruce Phillips of EcoPlan Associates, Inc., in Mesa, Arizona; and the faunal analysis was done by Kari Schmidt Cates, then a graduate student in the Department of Anthropology at the University of New Mexico. Dendrochronology samples were submitted to the Laboratory of Tree Ring Research at the University of Arizona in Tucson and radiocarbon samples were submitted to Beta Analytic Laboratory in Miami, Florida. Archaeomagnetic samples were collected and analyzed by William Deaver, then at Statistical Research Inc., in Tucson.

Additional excavations were done in Pithouse 8 in 2009 as part of UNLV's summer field school in the Mimbres Valley. This pithouse is an early Three Circle phase structure located in the central portion of site (Figure 2.2). The house was originally excavated in 2004 with a single 1-m by 2-m unit that was dug into the center of the house. The house burned. The excavated portion contained three partially reconstructible ceramic vessels (two Three Circle neck corrugated jars and one Three Circle Red-on-white bowl), an intentionally broken mortar, a pestle, and numerous cores (Roth 2010a). Permission to conduct additional

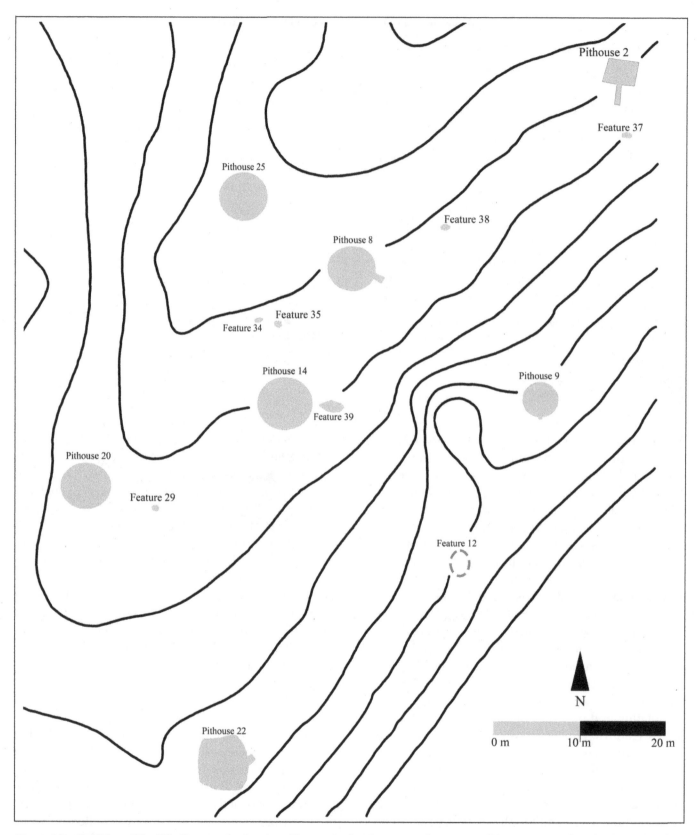

Figure 2.2. Site Map of La Gila Encantada showing all excavated pithouses and extramural features. Map by Elizabeth Toney and Danielle Romero.

excavations of Pithouse 8 was requested because the house had the potential to provide significant information to address the research questions for the project given that it had a relatively intact floor assemblage and dated to the early Three Circle phase (ca A.D. 750–775), a time period not represented by other excavated houses at the site.

Because the goals of these additional excavations were to expose the main portion of the house, it was excavated as a feature around the original 1-m by 2-m unit. The outline of the house was determined based on the presence of a shallow depression and excavations focused within the central portion of the structure. The feature was excavated using the methods used in the other houses at the site to ensure consistency and comparability in data collection. Because we had a sample of trash from the 2005 excavations that established a low density of trash deposits, only the first 30 cm of trash fill below the overburden was excavated in 10-cm arbitrary levels; the fill was sifted through ¼-inch mesh screen. The remainder of the trash fill was excavated without screening until roof fall was encountered; however, artifacts such as complete stone tools, ground stone, and possible reconstructible vessels were collected from the fill.

Extramural Excavations

One component of this project involved examining the extramural use of space to address the topic of household organization. Fourteen 1-m by 2-m units, one 1-m by 1-m unit, and one 1-m by 3-m unit were excavated outside of the excavated houses. Some of these units were placed outside the entryways of excavated houses so that materials found in the units could be linked with activities associated with the household occupying the structure. Previous work at Wind Mountain (Woosley and McIntyre 1996) and NAN Ranch (Shafer 2003) has shown that extramural features tend to be located from 1 to 3 meters in front of the a house's entryway. Nine extramural features (8 hearths and a midden) were identified (Table 2.2; Figure 2.2).

Originally, we anticipated that extramural features would be identified using magnetometer data. Unfortunately, this did not turn out to be the case at La Gila Encantada. Six 1-m by 2-m units were placed over magnetic anomalies on the site. Of these, two proved to be extramural features, one proved to be a burned pithouse (Unit 14, Pithouse 8), and three were sterile.

The extramural units were excavated in 10-cm arbitrary levels with all deposits screened through ¼-inch mesh. If features were encountered in these units, they were excavated separately, and all feature fill was screened through

Table 2.2. Excavated Extramural Features at La Gila Encantada

Feature Number	Unit Number	Feature Type	Location
12	25	Midden	Slope on east side of site
29		Extramural Hearth	Between Pithouses 20 and 28
30		Hearth	Pithouse 22 roof fall
34	20A	Extramural Hearth	Central portion of site
35	20	Extramural Hearth	Central portion of site
36	17, 18	Secondary Hearth	Pithouse 14
37	19, 22	Extramural Hearth	Outside Pithouse 2
38	16	Extramural Hearth	Outside Pithouse 6
39	37	Extramural Hearth	East of Pithouse 14

⅛-inch mesh screen. Flotation, pollen, and dating samples were taken from the fill of each feature.

No burials were found at La Gila Encantada and no communal structures (great kivas) were present, which differs significantly from the larger riverine sites in the Mimbres and Gila river valleys (Creel and Anyon 2003). Great kivas are readily apparent at ridge top pithouse sites because of their size and depth, so if one was present at La Gila Encantada, then it would have shown up as a surface depression or in the magnetometer survey. The lack of burials and great kivas was one of the factors used to assess the nature of social organization at La Gila Encantada and its relationship to other Late Pithouse period sites in the region.

EXCAVATION RESULTS—PITHOUSES

Seven pithouses were excavated during investigations at La Gila Encantada, with one dating to the Georgetown phase, one to the San Francisco phase, and three to the Three Circle phase (Figure 2.2; Table 2.1). Four pithouses were excavated in their entirety or nearly entirely (Pithouses 2, 8, 14, and 22 on Figure 2.2), one was tested using a 1-m by 3-m unit (Pithouse 9), and two houses (Pithouses 20 and 25) located on private land adjacent to the Archaeological Conservancy land on the west side of the site were bisected (Figure 2.2). One San Francisco phase structure (Pithouse 23) had been excavated previously during preliminary work at the site in 1998; unfortunately, no data were available on this structure with the exception of its assignment to the San Francisco phase.

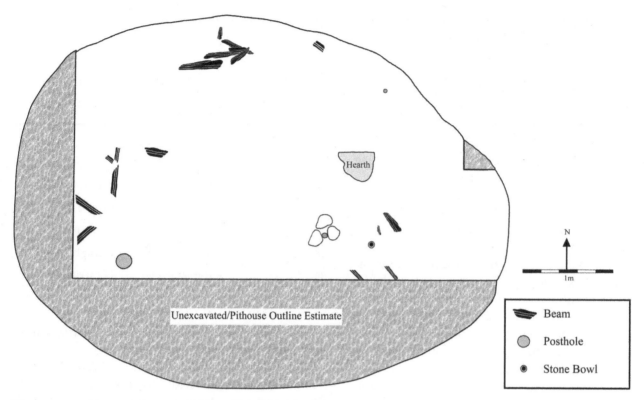

Figure 2.3. Pithouse 14 floor map showing excavated portion of the Georgetown phase structure with burned beams representing the roof that fell on the floor. The stone bowl/mortar was associated with a shell bracelet fragment and projectile point that have been interpreted as part of the ritual retirement of the house. Map by Danielle Romero.

Georgetown Phase Component—Pithouse 14

One Georgetown phase structure was excavated during fieldwork at La Gila Encantada. The pithouse was oval, measuring approximately 5 m by 5 m. It had a plastered floor and walls, and the hearth consisted of a layer of ash on a burned surface in the eastern portion of the structure (Figure 2.3). The identified postholes suggest that the house had a four-post support pattern with perimeter posts along the exterior walls. No entryway was found during excavations, but existing structural data indicate that the entryway faced south.

The house was intentionally burned after being cleaned out. Burned beams were found in the roof fall/wall fall and several burned beams were found on the floor, indicating that the roof fell directly onto the floor. A large quantity of ash was also noted in the floor fill. The house was then left open for some period of time and was later filled with trash. A secondary occupation consisting of a hearth and associated occupation surface was found in the trash fill above the roof fall (Feature 36) and most likely dates to the Three Circle phase. Figure 2.4 shows the stratigraphy of the deposits in Pithouse 14.

Two beams from Pithouse 14 yielded radiocarbon dates; one from A.D. 600 to 660 (one sigma) with an A.D. 640 intercept, the other from A.D. 380 to 530 (one sigma) with an A.D. 420 intercept (Table 2.1). The oval shape of the feature, lack of formal hearth, and the recovered ceramic assemblage (Alma Plain and scored redware) all indicate that this house dates to the Georgetown phase. Given the radiocarbon dates, it appears that it was occupied in the A.D. 500s or early 600s.

This house was unique in that the structure was ritually retired after abandonment, representing the first documented case of ritual retirement of a domestic structure in the Mimbres region (Roth and Schriever 2015). The ritual retirement involved the placement of a stone bowl/mortar containing corn pollen, an Early Archaic period stemmed point, and a fragment of a shell bracelet on the floor south of the hearth prior to the structure's burning. A second broken stone bowl/mortar was found in the floor fill directly above these artifacts. As discussed by Roth and Schriever (2015), this is similar to ritual retirement activities noted for communal structures in the Mimbres region by Creel and Anyon (2003). They argue that these

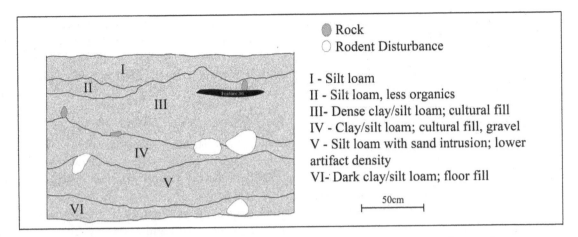

Figure 2.4. Stratigraphic profile of north wall of excavation unit of Georgetown phase Pithouse 14 showing Feature 36 (the dark lens), a secondary occupation in the trash fill of the house. Profile by Danielle Romero.

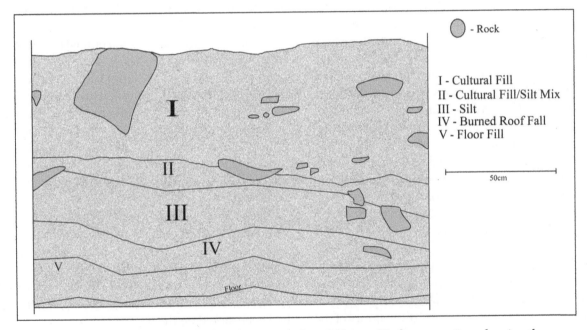

Figure 2.5. Profile of the west wall of San Francisco phase Pithouse 22 after excavation, showing the depth of the trash deposits in this house. Profile by Danielle Romero.

household rituals were important aspects of Mimbres lifeways, further indicating that La Gila Encantada was part of a larger Pithouse period identity in the Mimbres region.

San Francisco Phase Component—Pithouse 22

One San Francisco phase pithouse was excavated on the south end of the site (Figure 2.2). A trench had been dug through the center of the house during previous test excavations, so some disturbance was present. The test trench did not extend to the floor, however, so disturbance was confined to the upper fill of the house. The house burned after being left open for a period of time; it was incompletely burned and there was no evidence of charring of large beams or on the wall or floor plaster. Lenses of silt in the roof fall/wall fall indicate that material washed into the house as the walls were decomposing. The house was filled with a large quantity of trash, including ceramics, worked sherds, ground stone fragments, broken stone tools, and debitage. The density of trash and decorated ceramic styles indicate that the house was used for trash disposal during much of the Three Circle phase (Figure 2.5).

The house was rectangular with rounded corners, measured 4 m by 4.5 m, and had a stepped-ramp entryway that faced northeast (Figure 2.6). Based on the posthole pattern, the house had a three-post support on each side with a large center post and a series of perimeter posts. All of the wood used for posts was piñon or juniper; no other construction wood was found in the posthole samples. A burned piñon beam recovered from a floor storage pit dated to A.D. 679v (outer ring; inner ring 621 p) and a radiocarbon date from a burned beam on the floor had a one-sigma date of A.D. 640 to 690, with an intercept date of A.D. 660 (Table 2.1). These two dates place the house firmly in the San Francisco phase.

The collared basin hearth was filled with ash. A shallow ash pit was found behind the center post toward the back of the house; this is inferred to be an informal secondary hearth used to heat the back of the house. The presence of this feature and the storage pit described next suggest that the house was used by seasonally mobile San Francisco phase people who occupied the structure during the winter.

One storage pit was found along the north wall of the house. The pit was apparently open when the house burned and the roof fell, as fragments of burned beams were recovered from its fill. Juniper bark and pine needles were also recovered from the pit, indicating that it had been lined with those materials. A pollen wash from sherds recovered in the storage pit yielded abundant maize pollen (see Chapter 6), along with piñon, oak, and chenoams.

Numerous artifacts were recovered from the floor and floor fill of Pithouse 22; however, some of the artifacts represent a mixture of trash fill and floor fill. Artifacts in floor context include a broken metate with red ochre on it, a broken mano, a redware scoop, a figurine fragment, a complete core, several broken bifaces, and portions of several plainware and redware vessels. The majority of the materials recovered from floor contexts were in the front portion of the house near the hearth and near the storage pit; the back of the house contained very few artifacts. The metate, which appears to have been intentionally broken and then covered with red ochre, may have been part of the ritual closure of this house, although the situation is less clear than that associated with the ritual closure of the Georgetown phase structure (Pithouse 14).

Three Circle Phase Component—
Pithouses 2, 8, 9, 20, 25

Five of the excavated pithouses dated to the Three Circle phase (Table 2.1). These houses were more substantial architecturally than the Georgetown and San Francisco

phase houses and appear to have been associated with both population increase and increased sedentism at the site, although the results of the magnetometer survey and the confines of the ridgetop make it unlikely that the population living at the site was large.

Early Three Circle Component—Pithouse 8

The earliest Three Circle phase house, Pithouse 8, was located in the center of the site. It was tested during the 2005 field season with a 1-m by 2-m unit. Additional excavations of the interior of the house were done in 2009, revealing the front section of the house including the center post, hearth, and entryway. The size of the house could not be determined because only the east wall was uncovered. The walls were plastered, and the entryway was oriented to the southeast at 110 degrees. The hearth was an ash-filled basin with a hearth stone in line with the entryway (Figure 2.7).

The house burned and several burned beams were recovered during excavations. The house was at least partially intentionally filled after it burned. Much of the cultural fill had a very low artifact density and the sediments contained less sand and silt than the other houses, suggesting that it had not been left open in the same manner as the other houses. It may have been filled after the house burned to level the surface; however, it is also possible that the house was intentionally filled as part of the closure of the structure.

Six bone tools were found in the roof fall/wall fall, along with charcoal, ash, and a spindle whorl. These were apparently stored in the rafters of the house, although it is possible that they were stored on the roof. One mortar fragment and portions of a Three Circle Neck Corrugated jar were found in the roof fall/wall fall; it is likely that these had been stored on the roof.

A relatively intact assemblage was recovered from the plastered floor. Four ceramic vessels were found between the hearth and the center post hole. These included two partially reconstructible Three Circle neck-corrugated jars, a Three Circle Red-on-white bowl, and portions of a Mimbres Black-on-white Style I bowl. One spindle whorl and a ceramic scoop were also recovered. Five cores, one chert bifacial knife, three denticulates, a notch, and several retouched flakes were found in the floor fill and on the floor. Abundant ash was present along the wall near the entryway. The ash may have been the burned remains of a perishable artifact such as a basket. One large metate was leaning against the east wall to the north of the entryway. Two manos, one of which was compatible with the metate, were

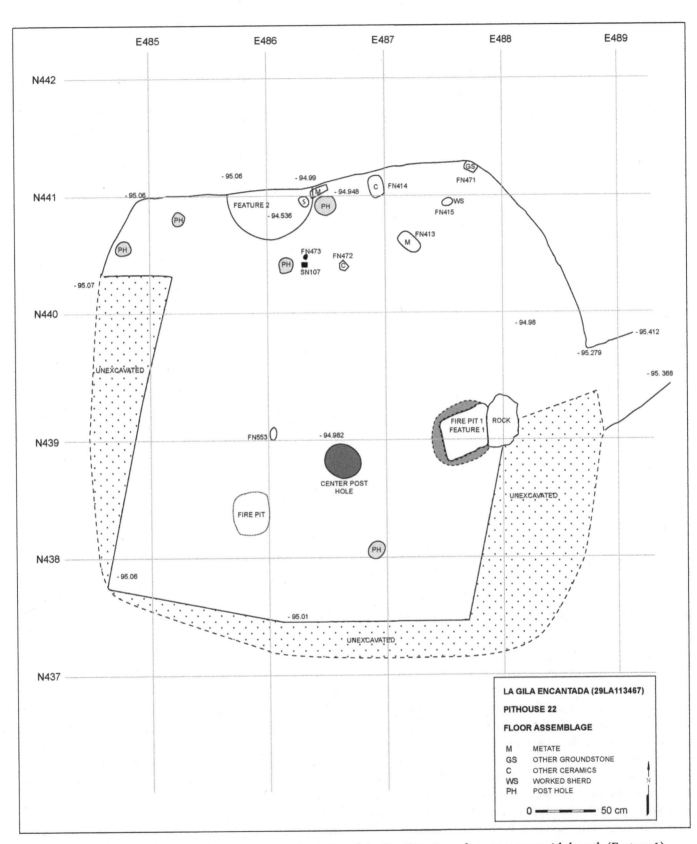

Figure 2.6. Pithouse 22 floor map showing excavated portion of the San Francisco phase structure with hearth (Feature 1), ash pit (fire pit behind hearth), center post, and storage pit (Feature 2). Map by Aaron Woods.

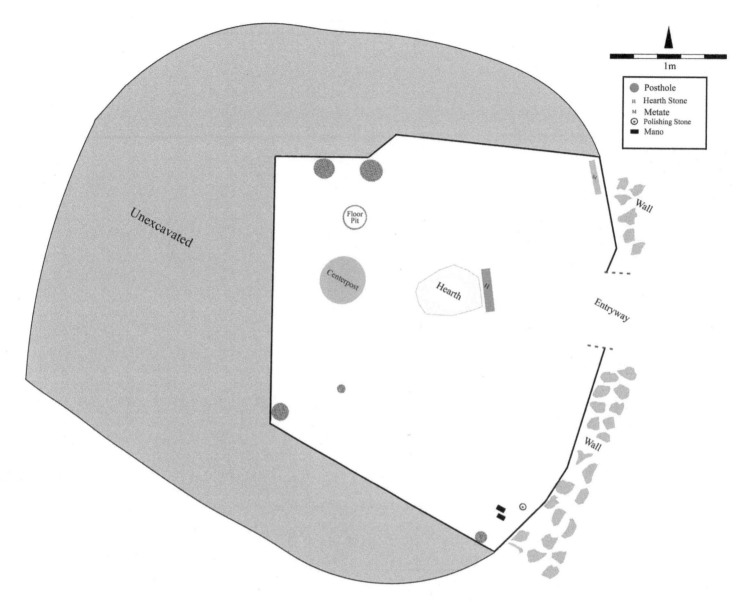

Figure 2.7. Pithouse 8 floor map showing excavated portion of early Three Circle phase structure. Map by Danielle Romero.

found stacked against the wall near the southeast corner of the house. A polishing stone was found with the manos.

In addition to the artifacts associated with domestic activities, numerous artifacts inferred to have been associated with ritual dedication and retirement activities were recovered. Five pieces of chrysocolla were found in the roof fall/wall fall and one piece was found in the floor fill, along with several mica fragments, a quartz crystal, a broken turquoise bead, and a piece of azurite. These materials have been shown by Roth and Schriever (2015) to be associated with household dedication and retirement rituals. One intentionally broken mortar with an associated

pestle was found. This was likely placed there during the final closure of the house.

A radiocarbon sample obtained from Pithouse 8 dated to A.D. 690 to 810 (one-sigma), with an intercept point of A.D. 770. This places it in the early Three Circle phase, which is supported by the recovery of portions of a Three Circle Red-on-white vessel on the floor.

Pithouse 2

This Three Circle phase house was located at the north end of the site (Figure 2.2). Given the large artifact assemblage on the floor, it appears that this house was accidentally

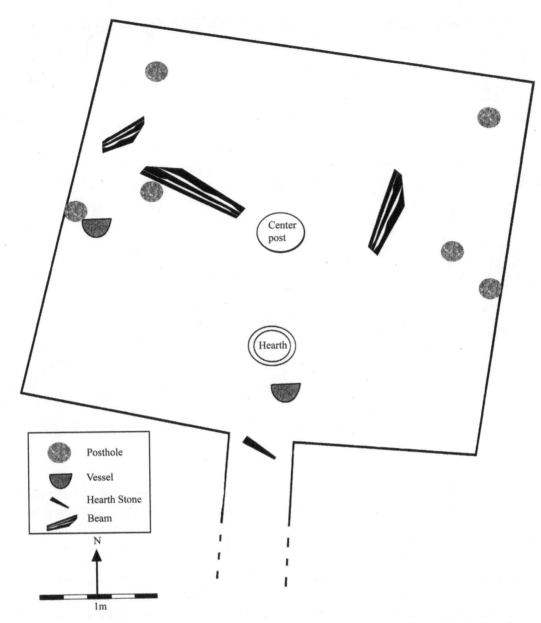

Figure 2.8. Pithouse 2 floor map showing location of burned beams in Three Circle phase house. Map by Danielle Romero.

burned and later filled with trash. It was rectangular, measured 4 m by 4 m, and had a lateral entryway that faced south (Figure 2.8). The walls were plastered and much of the wall plaster was preserved by the fire. It had a three-post support pattern with a large center post. It appears that the fire started in the hearth; one plainware jar was found overturned atop the hearth and may have fallen in during burning. The fire then spread to the post located in the southwest corner of the house (to the west of the entryway), burned along the west wall to the back and in the center of the house, and then along the northeast wall (Figure 2.9). The southeast portion of the house, located east of the entry, was not as heavily burned as the remainder of the house and was devoid of artifacts. Numerous burned beams were found in the roof fall/wall fall and on the floor. The roof fall also contained what appears to be a roof top assemblage consisting of a mano, an awl tip/flaker, a netherstone, a scraper, a core, numerous biface fragments, five worked sherds, and two polishing stones, indicating that the roof was used as an activity area.

Figure 2.9. Photo of Pithouse 2 floor after excavation, looking south toward entryway. Note burned plaster (white) on floor. Photo by Barbara Roth.

The floor was plastered and where the fire was hottest (hearth, west wall, center post), the floor and wall plaster had burned. Abundant ash was found throughout the floor fill and pockets of ash were found along the walls. The pockets may have been the remains of burned perishable materials such as baskets. The plaster-lined basin hearth was filled with ash. Remnants of the center post, an unknown conifer, were found in the posthole. The post was heavily insect-infested (McBride and Toll 2010).

A large number of artifacts were found on the floor attesting to the accidental nature of the fire. In general, Mimbres pithouses were cleaned of usable materials before they were abandoned (Diehl 1998; Roth 2015). The recovered household assemblage was important for reconstructing domestic activities at the site. Artifacts recovered from the floor included a metate that was stored along the wall east of the entryway, a common location for metate storage in Pithouse period houses (Roth 2010b). One plainware bowl, a small plainware jar, two neck-corrugated jars, and one Mimbres Black-on-white Style I bowl were found on the floor, along with portions of several other bowls and jars. The majority of the artifacts were found in the front portion of the house around the hearth, although one bowl and several piles of lithics, including numerous biface fragments and cores, were found along the western wall where they apparently had been stored. The back portion of the house was empty of artifacts, but contained abundant ash, suggesting that this area was used for sleeping and the burned ash may represent sleeping mats or other stored perishables. Surprisingly, no manos were found on the floor. The presence of ground stone in roof fall/wall fall as well as in an extramural feature (Feature 37) located directly in front of the entryway. indicate that grinding activities occurred outside. Given the artifact distributions, it appears that the house burned during the summer or perhaps early fall when most of the activities took place outdoors and the house was used primarily for some food preparation, sleeping, and storage.

One burned roof beam from Pithouse 2 was radiocarbon-dated to A.D. 660 to 710 (one sigma), with an intercept date of A.D. 680. A second beam dated from A.D. 790 to 900, with an intercept date of A.D. 880. Burned wall plaster from Pithouse 2 yielded an archaeomagnetic date with a best-of-fit date of A.D. 825 (Table 2.1). The ceramic and architectural data place the house in the Three Circle phase, but the lack of Three Circle Red-on-white pottery indicates that it most likely post-dates A.D. 775. Mimbres Black-on-white Style I was predominant in the floor fill of the house and a Mimbres Black-on-white Style I bowl and scoop were found on the floor. Given the radiocarbon, archaeomagnetic, and ceramic dates, it appears that the house was occupied and burned in the early to mid-800s, although this remains the most insecurely dated of all the houses at La Gila Encantada, a surprising fact given the fact that it burned catastrophically.

Pithouse 9

This Three Circle phase house was located on the east side of the site; it had a small, shallow looter's hole dug into the surface depression. The looter activity was confined to the upper trash fill and did not extend to the roof fall or floor. This house was tested with a 1-m by 3-m unit that exposed the hearth, center post, and entryway. The house burned, but not completely, probably after a period of abandonment, as alluvial deposits had washed into the house before the roof and walls collapsed. Little trash was present in the fill.

The hearth was a large, plastered basin filled with ash. The entryway faced south-southwest. The center post was removed prior to abandonment and the house was cleaned out, indicating that it was a planned abandonment. A burned beam from Pithouse 9 yielded one-sigma radiocarbon dates of A.D. 810–840, 860–910, and 920–960, with a two-sigma range of A.D. 780 to 980 and an intercept at A.D. 890 (Table 2.1). Because the house was cleaned out before abandonment, left open for a period of time, and later looted, the ceramic data are less clearly associated with this house than the other pithouses. The presence of Mimbres Black-on-white Style I in the floor fill supports a mid-Three Circle phase date but does not preclude a late A.D. 800s date. An archaeomagnetic sample from the hearth dated from A.D. 835 to 1015. The lack of trash fill supports a later occupation date.

Pithouse 20

This house was located on the west side of the site and was partially excavated with two adjacent 2-m by 2-m units (32, 33) placed on the west side of the house. The house was cleaned out, abandoned, and then burned at some later time after the roof and walls had started to collapse. Several artifacts found in the roof fall/wall fall may have been materials left on the roof when the house was abandoned. These included a mortar, a broken metate, a large mano,

and a polishing stone. The hearth and entryway were not encountered in the test units.

Only seven sherds, one metate fragment, and several pieces of debitage were recovered from the floor. No datable materials were recovered from the house, but ceramic data, including several Mimbres Black-on-white Style II sherds in the roof fall, indicate that the house may date to the late Three Circle phase, either the late A.D. 800s or early 900s.

Pithouse 25

This house was located on the northwest side of the site (Figure 2.2); it was bisected with two adjacent 2-m by 2-m units. The house burned after being partially cleaned out and several burned beams were recovered from the roof fall. The floor was plastered and burned in places where burned beams fell. The hearth was a shallow basin lined with plaster and filled with ash (Figure 2.10).

Numerous artifacts were found on the floor, many of them around the hearth. These included three manos, one metate fragment, a core, a chopper/hammerstone, a pecking stone, and a denticulate. The recovered assemblage points to processing activities within the house. One small Mimbres Black-on-white Style I bowl was found in the floor fill near the north wall of the house, but no other ceramic vessels were found. Given the prevalence of vessels recovered around the hearth of Pithouses 2 and 8, it appears that most of the ceramic vessels were removed prior to the house burning.

A burned roof beam from Pithouse 25 yielded a one-sigma radiocarbon date of A.D. 770 to 900, with intercepts at A.D. 810, 840, and 860 (Table 2.1). As noted previously, a Mimbres Black-on-white Style I vessel was found in the floor fill, which indicates that the house dates to the early to mid-800s.

EXCAVATION RESULTS—EXTRAMURAL FEATURES

Nine extramural features were excavated at the site, the majority of which were hearths (Table 2.2). These features and their associated artifact assemblages illustrate that much of the daily domestic processing activities took place outside the houses. Six extramural hearths were found, three of which could be associated with specific pithouses and thus can be linked to household activities. Two small extramural hearths were found near each other (Features 34 and 35); these may represent a communally used extramural work area, as they were not associated with particular houses.

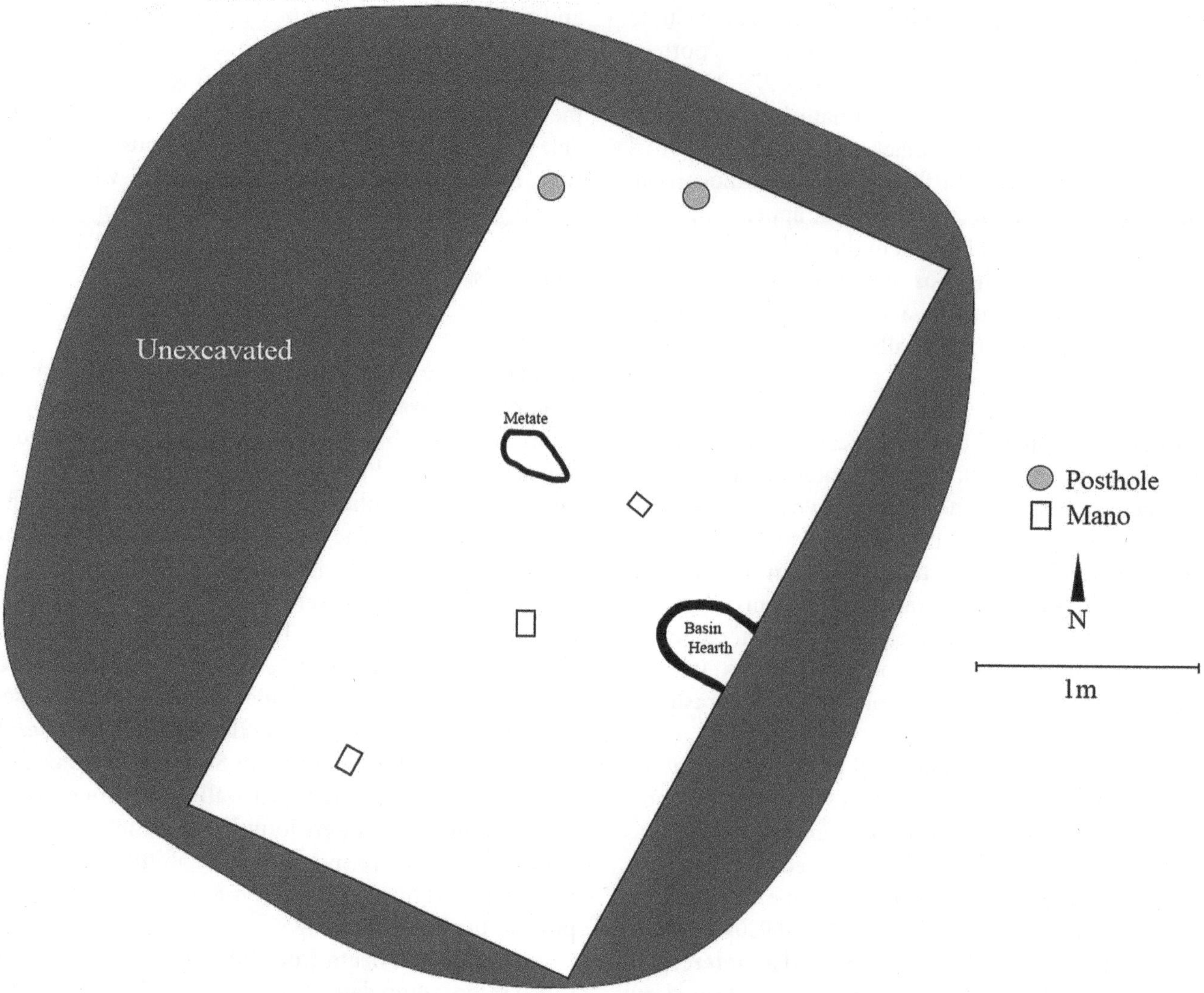

Figure 2.10. Pithouse 25 floor map showing excavated portion of the Three Circle phase structure. Excavations were done in the center portion of the house so the entryway was not located. Map by Danielle Romero.

Similar artifacts were associated with the extramural hearths including ground stone, cores, and chipped stone tools. Maize cupules were recovered from four of them, indicating that maize processing occurred outdoors. One small basin hearth (Feature 37) was found outside burned Pithouse 2 and provided further evidence of household activities. The hearth was associated with a compact use surface that contained two cores, two core fragments, two choppers, a polishing stone, a stone palette fragment, seven biface fragments, two broken unifaces, and a two-hand trough mano. A flotation sample from the hearth yielded maize and a purslane seed. These data and those from the other extramural hearths indicate the flint knapping and food processing occurred outside the houses.

In addition to the hearths, one shallow (40-cm deep) midden was found on a slight slope in the east-central portion of the site (Feature 12). The midden fill contained many artifacts, including stone tools, debitage, many plain-ware and decorated ceramics, and mule deer and cottontail rabbit bones. The decorated wares spanned the Pithouse period, including Mogollon Red-on-brown, Three Circle Red-on-white, Mimbres Black-on-white Style I (Boldface) and Style I/II. Given the shallow depth of the midden, it appears that this represents sheet trash rather than formal trash deposition. Abandoned pithouses appear to have been used for most trash deposition at the site.

Two of the pithouses had secondary occupations that were extramural features for other households. Both were found in earlier pithouses on the site and likely represent Three Circle phase re-use of the structures. Feature 36 was an extramural hearth on a compact surface situated in the roof fall/wall fall of Georgetown phase Pithouse 14. Several cores and core fragments were found in the level near the feature and were likely associated with it. Feature 30 was found in the roof fall/wall fall of San Francisco phase Pithouse 22 and had a hearth, associated metate, and compact surface. The hearth was small and circular with some ash and charcoal, but it does not appear to have been heavily used. The metate was very lightly ground. Several cores were found in the level near this feature and were apparently associated with it.

SUMMARY

Excavations at La Gila Encantada resulted in the recovery of seven pithouses dating to all phases of the Late Pithouse period and nine extramural features. These data provided information on household activities of the site occupants, the nature of the occupation, and the formation processes involved in house abandonment. The recovered data indicate that the houses were discrete and thus likely independent; no evidence of clusters of households were found, as has been documented at pithouse sites in the Mimbres River Valley (Creel 2006; Shafer 2003; Roth 2019b). No burials were found in any of the excavated houses. Ritual activities are indicated by the ritual retirement of the Georgetown phase structure and possibly the closure of San Francisco phase Pithouse 22. The lack of great kivas suggests that these activities were not part of larger-scale communal rituals. If those occurred, they took place elsewhere, perhaps at one of the larger pithouse sites in the area. The insights gained from the architectural data were enhanced by more detailed analysis of the artifacts and subsistence remains recovered from the houses and extramural features; these are described in the following chapters.

CHAPTER THREE

Ceramic Data

Barbara J. Roth, Danielle Romero, Thomas E. Gruber, Christina Dykstra, and Linda M. Gregonis

This chapter presents the results of the analysis of plainware, decorated ware, and worked ceramics recovered during excavations at La Gila Encantada. The decorated wares were analyzed by Thomas Gruber (2004, 2005 seasons) and Danielle Romero (whole vessels); plainware, corrugated, and redwares were analyzed by Christina Dykstra; and worked sherds were analyzed by Linda Gregonis. The analysis focused on attributes that would provide information on chronology, household activities, and social interaction, specifically to address research questions concerning subsistence practices and household organization.

DECORATED CERAMICS

The decorated ceramic assemblage from La Gila Encantada included 1,140 sherds recovered during the 2004 and 2005 field seasons. Analysis focused on the types of wares present, any differences or similarities across the pithouses, and use-wear present on the sherds. Sample sizes differed significantly among the household assemblages. Ceramic data were most comprehensive for Pithouses 2, 14 and 22; site-level comparisons were made using data from these pithouses.

Analysis Methods

Previous research on Mimbres ceramics has focused on the painted wares and has been based on changes in design styles over time. The methods used for this analysis drew on previous typological work by Cosgrove and Cosgrove (1932) and Haury (1936) that was later refined by Anyon and LeBlanc (1984) and Shafer and Brewington (1995). Ceramics from the Late Pithouse period include Mogollon Red-on-brown,

which is currently dated from A.D. 650 to 750 (see Anyon and others 2017 for a discussion of on-going revisions of the current chronology); Three Circle Red-on-white, which is dated from A.D. 730 to 770; Mimbres Black-on-white Style I (Boldface Black-on-white), which dates from the late A.D. 700s to the late 800s; and Mimbres Black-on-white Style II (Mangas Black-on-white), which was produced from A.D. 880 to 1020. The Classic period ceramics are Classic Mimbres Black-on-white Style III, which dates from A.D. 1010 to 1130, and Mimbres Polychrome, which dates from A.D. 1060 to 1130. Although these are the main types of painted ceramics found in the Mimbres region, it is sometimes difficult to assign sherds to one of these types.

Eleven categories were used to classify the painted sherds from La Gila Encantada (Gruber and others 2010). These represent the painted types, indeterminate types between known types, indeterminate Mimbres Black-on-white sherds, and non-Mimbres painted types. A ceramic typed as indeterminate between two known types represented a sherd that did not have enough characteristics to place it in any single category but had enough characteristics to place it in one of two temporally consecutive categories (e.g., Mimbres Black-on-white Style I/II). The other painted white wares were non-Mimbres painted ceramics that were apparently obtained through trade.

Other attributes recorded during the analysis included vessel form, temper, and use wear characteristics including scraping and weathering. Where possible, rim diameter was estimated for a comparison of vessel sizes.

Painted Ceramic Assemblage

Overall, the most common decorated type recovered at La Gila Encantada was an indeterminate Mimbres

Table 3.1. Decorated Ceramic Types from the 2004 and 2005 Seasons

Ceramic Type	Number (%) of Sherds
Indeterminate Black-on-white	506 (44)
Mimbres Black-on-white Style I (Boldface)	254 (22)
Mimbres Black-on-white Style II (Mangas)	66 (6)
Mimbres Black-on-white Style III (Classic)	6 (<1)
Mimbres Black-on-white Style I/II	164 (14)
Mimbres Black-on-white Style II/III	8 (<1)
Three Circle Red-on-white/Mimbres Black-on-white Style I	17 (1)
Three Circle Red-on-white	80 (7)
Mogollon Red-on-brown	17 (1)
Other decorated	13 (1)
Total Number of Sherds	**1140**

Decorated Ceramic Data by Pithouse

Table 3.2 presents the ceramic sherd data from Pithouses 2, 14, and 22, which contained the bulk of the decorated wares recovered during excavations. Four additional pithouses were excavated (Pithouses 8, 9, 20, 25) but data from them are not directly comparable to the other pithouses because of the small samples obtained, so they were not included in site-level comparisons.

Pithouse 2. Pithouse 2 had 334 decorated sherds; one complete Mimbres Black-on-white Style I bowl was recovered from the floor. Pithouse 2 roof fall/wall fall ceramic frequencies are similar to the site averages, with indeterminate black-on-white sherds dominating the assemblage, followed by inderminate Mimbres Black-on-white Style I/II and Mimbres Black-on-white Style I (Table 3.2).

Pithouse 2 floor context ceramic frequencies are similar to the overall site averages, with indeterminate black-on-white ceramics most frequent in floor fill and on the floor (Table 3.2). Mimbres Black-on-white Style I (Boldface) ceramics represent the next most frequent type with 34 percent, followed by Indeterminate Mimbres Black-on-white Style I/II at 11 percent. Three Circle Red-on-white (6%) and Mimbres Black-on-white Style II (6%) were recovered in lower numbers. A higher percentage of Mimbres Black-on-white Style I (Boldface) ceramics was present in this house than in the other excavated houses, which is supported by dating samples from the house (see Chapter 2) that place the structure in the early to mid-Three Circle phase.

Pithouse 14. Pithouse 14 had 85 decorated ceramics, the vast majority of which (95%; N=81) were found in trash fill. The ceramic data support other data that indicate the house collapsed, filled naturally, and was then filled with trash. Most ceramics in the trash fill were indeterminate

Black-on-white category (Gruber and others 2010), in which not enough of a design was present to conclusively determine one type over the other. This type accounts for 44 percent of the decorated sherd assemblage (Table 3.1). This was followed by Mimbres Black-on-white Style I (Boldface) (22%), Indeterminate Mimbres Black-on-white Style I/II (14%) and Mimbres Black-on-white Style II (Mangas) (7%). The remaining sherds accounted for less than 2 percent of the assemblage and included 17 Mogollon Red-on-brown, 5 Cibola white wares (determined by white kaolin clay paste), and 7 sherds with a white slip but no visible paint. These sherd data support the chronometric dates and indicate that the main occupation of the site falls within the early to mid-Three Circle phase.

Table 3.2. Decorated Sherds by Pithouse

Ceramic Type	Pithouse 2 Number (%)	Pithouse 14 Number (%)	Pithouse 22 Number (%)
Indeterminate Black-on-white	126 (38)	51 (60)	218 (43)
Mimbres Black-on-white Style I	77 (23)	14 (16)	117 (23)
Mimbres Black-on-white Style II	22 (7)	4 (5)	31 (6)
Mimbres Black-on-white Style III	1 (<1)	0	4 (<1)
Three Circle Red-on-white	25 (7)	3 (3)	38 (7)
Mogollon Red-on-brown	2 (<1)	2 (2)	7 (4)
Other decorated	15 (5)	0	2 (<1)
Total Number of Sherds	**334**	**85**	**500**

black-on-white (62%), followed by Mimbres Black-on-white Style I (17%), and Indeterminate Mimbres Black-on-white Style I/II (9%). This suggests that the house was filled with trash during the Three Circle phase. No decorated wares were found on the floor. Ceramics recovered from the floor consisted exclusively of plainwares and redwares, which is consistent with the Georgetown phase date for the house.

Pithouse 22. Pithouse 22 had 500 decorated sherds (Table 3.2). Most of the decorated sherds from this house (81%) fall into the indeterminate black-on-white, Mimbres Black-on-white Style I, and indeterminate Mimbres Black-on-white Style I/II categories. It is important to evaluate the recovery context of the ceramics, however, as the vast majority (95%) came from trash fill and roof fall/wall fall contexts. The house was large and contained abundant trash fill, so the distribution of decorated wares appears to be associated primarily with the deposition of Three Circle phase trash. The house collapsed over time, which suggests that many of the ceramics in the roof fall/wall fall are also likely from trash deposits.

Floor context ceramic frequencies are similar to the site averages, despite the fact that the house is securely dated to the San Francisco phase with both a tree ring date and a radiocarbon date (see Chapter 2). This is the result of both the presence of abundant trash fill and disturbance by a previously dug trench. The frequencies may also be tied to the low overall number (N = 22) of decorated ceramics recovered from floor contexts. Indeterminate black-on-white ceramics (6 sherds) were most frequent in floor fill and floor contexts. Indeterminate Mimbres Black-on-white Style I/II sherds were the next most frequent, making up 23 percent of the sample (N = 5), followed by Mimbres Black-on-white Style 1 (N = 4; 18%), Mogollon Red-on-brown (N = 3; 14%), and Three Circle Red-on-white (N = 2; 9%). Despite the very small sample sizes, floor contexts from this house contained the highest percentage of Mogollon Red-on-brown of any of the houses, in keeping with the date of the house (ca A.D. 640).

Other Pithouses. Few decorated sherds were recovered from the other pithouses excavated during this project, or, as in the case of Pithouse 9, the context of the decorated ceramics could not be securely tied to the occupation of the house. These pithouses are discussed separately because the sherd data are not directly comparable to the excavated houses just discussed, and they were not included in site-level comparisons.

Of the 68 decorated sherds recovered from Pithouse 8 during the 2004 and 2005 seasons, 36 were from critical household contexts. Mimbres Black-on-white Style I was represented by 12 sherds, 8 of which were recovered from floor fill. The floor fill also included seven indeterminate Mimbres Black-on-white Style I/II and six Mimbres Black-on-white Style II sherds. Only four decorated sherds were recovered from the floor (one Mimbres Black-on-white Style I, one Three Circle Red-on-white, and two indeterminate black-on-white). Two reconstructible decorated vessels were recovered from the floor during the 2004 and 2009 field seasons; these are described later in this chapter.

Pithouse 25 had 10 decorated sherds, the smallest sample of decorated wares recovered from any of the houses. Unlike the site averages, however, no indeterminate black-on-white sherds were recovered from this house. The most frequent ceramic type was indeterminate Mimbres Black-on-white Style I/II (5 sherds), followed by Mimbres Black-on-white Style 1 (2 sherds), and Mimbres Black-on-white Style II (2 sherds). One sherd of Three Circle Red-on-white was found. These data, along with a complete Mimbres Black-on-white Style I vessel recovered from the floor fill support the radiocarbon dating of this house to the mid-Three Circle phase, with trash fill dating to the mid- to late Three Circle phase.

A 1-m by 3-m unit was excavated in Pithouse 9. The feature had been cleaned out prior to abandonment, was left open, and later looted. As a result, the contexts of the ceramics from this house were less secure than those from other structures. Excavations yielded 106 decorated sherds, the majority of which (77%) were found in cultural fill. Indeterminate black-on-white sherds represented the highest percentage of this type found at the site (54%; N = 57). Mimbres Black-on-white Style I sherds were next most common (26%; N = 28), with other types found in low numbers.

Pithouse 20 was cleaned out before it was abandoned, so ceramic data from this house are primarily from trash fill and sheet wash. Twenty-seven decorated sherds were recovered, the majority of which (78%) were from cultural fill. Indeterminate black-on-white sherds were the most common (52%; N = 14), including one found on the floor that was the only decorated ware found on the floor of this house. Other types represented in the sherd assemblage include Three Circle Red-on-white (N = 4), Mimbres Black-on-white Style I (N = 3), indeterminate Mimbres Black-on-white Style I/II (N = 2), and one sherd each of Mogollon Red-on-brown, Mimbres Black-on-white Style

II, Indeterminate Mimbres Black-on-white Style II/III, and Cibola whiteware. The mix of sherds recovered from this house may be due to the location of the house on a slight slope on the west edge of the site. The house was left open after it was abandoned and trash from the surface likely washed into it.

Decorated Vessel Types

A comparison of jar versus bowl sherds was done to address two questions: (1) are a variety of decorated vessel types present in the floor assemblages of the houses and (2) are there differences in the vessels between floor, roof fall/wall fall, and trash fill contexts? Data from all contexts from Pithouses 2, 8, 14, 22, and 25 were used in the analysis using a sample of 277 bowl and 62 jar sherds. The designation of jar versus bowl was made based on vessel shape, rim characteristics, and decoration location.

The data clearly show a preponderance of bowls in the decorated assemblage, with a 5-to-1 bowl to jar ratio. Surprisingly, the majority of bowls were not recovered from floor contexts; more bowl sherds were found in the roof fall/wall fall and cultural fill than in floor contexts. However, the two complete decorated bowls and one partially reconstructible decorated bowl were found in floor contexts.

Decorated jars were rarely recovered in house floor contexts; only two decorated jar sherds were found in the floor fill of Pithouse 2. Decorated jars were primarily found in roof fall/wall fall contexts, which indicate that they were either stored on the roofs or used in extramural activities on roof tops.

Use Wear Analysis

Use wear was examined by Danielle Romero for 936 of the decorated sherds from all pithouses, including the 2009 sherds from Pithouse 8. Attributes examined included scraping, pitting, weathering, and sooting.

Use wear in the form of erosion from use was present on the majority (N = 620; 66%) of the sherds. Although the amount of this type of wear varied from small thermal spalls to nearly 100 percent removal of the paint and slip, the large percentage of sherds exhibiting erosion is interesting. These data suggest that decorated ceramics were more heavily used than what has been observed at other Mimbres Pithouse period sites, perhaps indicating that they had a different, more extensive role in household activities than at other contemporary sites. This pattern of heavy use on decorated wares was mirrored in the whole vessels.

PLAINWARE, CORRUGATED, AND REDWARE CERAMICS

The focus of the analysis of plainware, corrugated, and redware ceramics was to address household organization. Christina Dykstra analyzed the plainware, corrugated, and redware ceramics from the 2004 and 2005 seasons. Following Rice (1987), attributes recorded include ware type (brownware, redware, corrugated, whiteware, other), vessel shape (bowl, jar), temper, presence and type of use wear, and rim diameter (if applicable). Ceramic distributions on pithouse floors were used to gain insights into activity areas, household organization, and the function of plainware and corrugated ceramic types.

Technically, all Mimbres Mogollon ceramics are brownwares. Within the non-painted brownware categories, three series were represented in the La Gila Encantada ceramic assemblage: plain brownware (Alma Plain), textured/corrugated brownware, and red-slipped brownware. Ten thousand two hundred twenty-three plainware, textured/corrugated, and redware sherds were analyzed from all excavated contexts at La Gila Encantada. This section summarizes the results, with more detailed data available in Gruber and others (2010).

Brownwares

Alma Plain represents the most common ceramic type found at La Gila Encantada, comprising 77 percent of the analyzed assemblage, although this probably includes sherds from vessels that were partially textured. Brownwares were predominant in all excavated contexts at the site, including cultural (trash) fill, roof fall/wall fall, floor fill, and extramural contexts. Ninety-two percent of the brownwares had some degree of exterior finishing, ranging from smoothed to highly polished. Alma Black Burnished was produced by polishing the exterior and interior of a vessel and then firing it in an atmosphere that drove burned organics (smoke) into the surface, leaving a black surface with a great deal of luster. The type was very rare at La Gila Encantada, accounting for less than 1 percent of the recovered assemblage. The majority of Alma Black Burnished sherds (N = 4) were found in the floor fill or floor of Pithouse 14, consistent with the Georgetown phase date of the house, and in the fill of Feature 29, an extramural hearth (N = 3) that was situated between Pithouses 20 and 28.

Corrugated Wares

Corrugated wares are those with surface treatments that change the texture of a vessel's surface, usually when the coils used to form the vessel are not completely smoothed. Haury's (1936) original pottery typology described changes in corrugation that occurred over time in terms of vessel coverage. The amount of corrugation increased to cover the upper third of the vessel during the Three Circle phase, marking the transition to Three Circle Neck Corrugated. By the Classic Mimbres period, corrugation began to cover the entire vessel (Anyon and LeBlanc 1984). For this analysis, different corrugation types were identified to determine if different proportions of these types were present within the ceramic assemblage, but with limited success. As a result, data interpretations rely primarily on the presence or absence of corrugation present.

A small portion of the sherd assemblage (6%) exhibited corrugation. This low percentage is most likely tied to the fact that corrugation was primarily located around the necks of jars during the Late Pithouse period and did not cover the entire vessel. Higher percentages of corrugated wares have been recovered from riverine pithouse sites (Anyon and LeBlanc 1984; Roth 2015). The low percentage from La Gila Encantada may be tied to differences in agricultural production and sedentism, with less production of large storage jars with neck corrugation at La Gila Encantada than at the larger, more sedentary, and more agriculturally focused riverine villages.

Redwares

Redwares made up 16 percent of the La Gila Encantada assemblage. Anyon and LeBlanc (1984) divided redwares into two different types: San Francisco Red, a formal, red-slipped ware that is usually highly polished and often exhibits dimpling on its surface, and miscellaneous red, a less finely executed and polished, red-slipped ware. For this analysis, no distinction was made between San Francisco Red and miscellaneous red, although both are represented in the ceramic assemblage. Many redwares (89%) exhibited exterior finishing (smoothing or polishing) and some were very highly polished, suggesting that San Francisco Red comprised the bulk of the assemblage. All redwares recovered from the floor and floor fill of Pithouse 14, the Georgetown phase structure, had been finished, traits consistent with the dating of this structure.

Whitewares

A small number of undecorated whitewares (N = 58; less than 1%) were part of the La Gila Encantada plainware assemblage. These had a white paste and were not locally produced, but no sourcing analysis was done, so their production location cannot be determined. Given their paste color and texture, it appears that most are either Cibola whitewares from north of the Mimbres region or white wares from the nearby West Fork of the Gila River. The overall low percentage of whitewares and absence of other nonlocal wares in the ceramic assemblage suggest that interaction outside the Mimbres region was not a major factor in everyday life at La Gila Encantada.

Context

The percentages of brown, corrugated, and redwares in the ceramic assemblage were very similar for all of the pithouse contexts. Cultural fill and roof fall/wall fall contexts were virtually identical (78% brownware, 6% corrugated, 15% redware) supporting the inference that these contexts represent trash deposition throughout the Three Circle phase occupation. Extramural contexts had a higher percentage of redwares (25%), but a low percentage of corrugated wares (6%).

An evaluation of wares by pithouse floor fill and floor contexts showed some differences among houses. As expected given its date, Pithouse 14 had the highest percentage of redware (22%). Pithouse 22 also had a higher percentage (18%), as did Pithouse 8 (20%). As these are the earliest houses on the site, the higher percentage of redware recovered from these earlier houses suggests that redware use may have decreased over time, a pattern noted by Shafer (2003) at NAN Ranch. However, the fact that redware is more common in extramural contexts may instead indicate that redware was used more often outside during the Three Circle phase.

Vessel Shape

Vessel shape was recorded for most sherds using rims, curvature, and location of the finish. Because of the difficulty in determining shape on body sherds, the analysis of jars versus bowls was done using only rim sherds. Both bowls and jars were well-represented in the sample, with jars slightly more common (52%) than bowls (48%). When broken down by wares, the ratios reveal some interesting patterns. More brownware sherds are from jars (63%) than bowls (37%); this is likely due to the use of jars for storage. In contrast, redware bowl sherds are much more common (79%) than jars (21%), indicating that they were primarily used for serving.

When the jar-to-bowl ratio is evaluated by context, some patterns in terms of discard and use are apparent. The jar and bowl percentages remain similar to the site percentages in cultural fill contexts. Roof fall/wall fall contains a slightly higher percentage of jars, perhaps because some roofs were used as work areas or jars were stored on roofs. Bowls are slightly more common than jars in floor fill but are much more common on floors (68%). The presence of jars in floor contexts indicates that some in-house storage and possibly cooking occurred. Extramural contexts contained substantially more jars than bowls. This supports other site data indicating that extramural areas were used for food processing and cooking activities.

Jar rim diameters increased through time. For example, Three Circle phase Pithouse 25 had almost three times as many rim sherds that represented a rim diameter of 15 cm or more than Georgetown phase Pithouse 14. This suggests that storage vessels became larger over time, likely as a response to increasing agricultural surpluses that came about due to an increasing dependence on agricultural production.

Use Wear

Use wear was examined on sherds located on the floor or in floor fill to obtain information on household activities. All sherds from floor fill and 97 percent of the sherds recovered from pithouse floors with signs of use wear had soot on the surface of the vessel, indicative of cooking activities. Sherds from several extramural hearths were also analyzed and the use wear results indicate that cooking activities took place in these hearths.

No functional differences in the plain, corrugated, and redware assemblages could be discerned among the different structures excavated at the site. The same cooking and storage activities were apparently carried out in all the structures. These data support other site data that suggest that a suite of domestic activities took place within households. Ceramic assemblages within pithouses indicate that the interior spaces of structures were used for storage and possibly food preparation and serving, while most cooking was done outside.

WHOLE OR RECONSTRUCTIBLE VESSELS

Nineteen whole and reconstructible vessels were recovered from the site. They include decorated, plainware, and corrugated pieces. Instrumental neutron activation analysis (INAA) was conducted on 13 of these vessels as part of a larger study of Mimbres region ceramic production.

Decorated Vessels

Eight decorated whole or reconstructible vessels were found during excavations at La Gila Encantada. The vessels were analyzed by Danielle Romero and included two complete bowls, five partially reconstructible bowls, and one

jar. Analysis focused on design style and layout; exterior finishes such as fire-clouding or sooting, smoothing, polishing, and burnishing; and rim characteristics including diameter and eversion. Interior attributes included sooting that resulted from cooking practices, polishing/burnishing, pitting, and scraping.

Both exterior and interior attributes were used to infer the potential use of the vessel. These included rim/orifice diameter and eversion, neck restriction, overall size (body diameter and height), volume of the vessel when full, shape, internal usewear (scraping, thermal spalling, and residues), surface treatment, and appendages such as handles (Hally 1986; Henrickson and McDonald 1983; Rice 1987; Sinopoli 1991). Using these attributes, vessels were then assigned to the following categories: dry or wet storage, food preparation, cooking (food preparation with added heat), dry or liquid serving, and transportation.

Two decorated bowls were recovered from Pithouse 2. One Mimbres Black-on-white Style I bowl was found on the floor along the west wall of the house (Figure 3.1). This bowl is small, measuring 7.1 cm in diameter and 3.5 cm in depth. The vessel is poorly executed in both manufacture and design and, like the bowl recovered from Pithouse 25

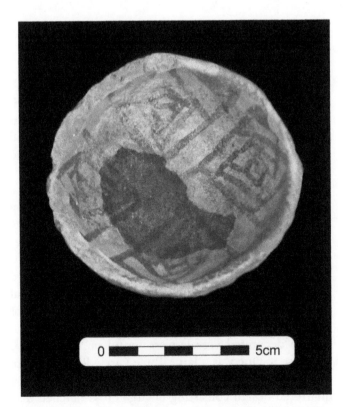

Figure 3.1. Mimbres Black-on-white Style I bowl from the floor of Pithouse 2. Photo by Danielle Romero.

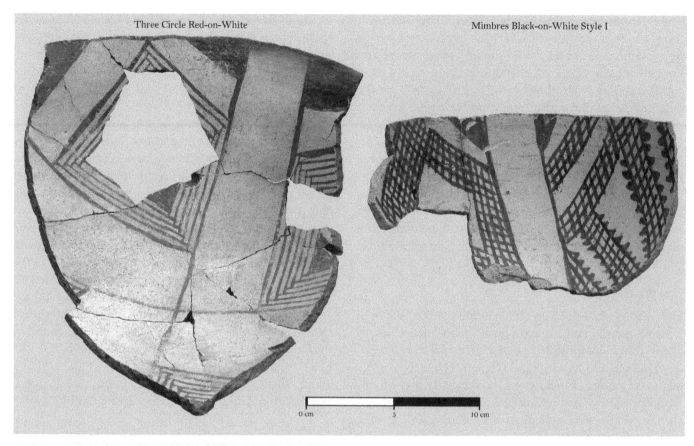

Three Circle Red-on-White

Mimbres Black-on-White Style I

0 cm   5   10 cm

Figure 3.2. Three Circle Red-on-white bowl (left) and Mimbres Black-on-white Style 1 bowl (right) from Pithouse 8. Photo by Danielle Romero.

discussed later, it is inferred to represent a child's or beginning potter's vessel (Crown 2001, 2002). Heavy wear was present on the interior including scraping, burning, and minor weathering. The exterior was not smoothed and there was evidence of blackening at the base.

The second decorated bowl from Pithouse 2 was a Mimbres Black-on-white Style I from a possible roof top work surface. It was well-made and heavily weathered. The design covers the entire interior surface and terminates into the rim. The vessel had a rim diameter of 16 cm and was rather shallow, with a depth of 8 cm. A large, blackened area was present on the exterior; it matches the natural resting state of the vessel, suggesting that it was on the roof when the house burned.

Two decorated vessels were found on the floor of Pithouse 8. One was a large Three Circle Red-on-white bowl found near the hearth (Figure 3.2). The bowl has a quartered design consisting of large cross-hatched diamond shapes that intersect at the center of the vessel, a design motif common for this style. Although the rim was

irregular in shape, rim diameter is estimated at 30 cm. The bowl was relatively shallow, with a depth of 12 cm. The exterior was unslipped and smoothed, but not polished. Use-wear evident on the bowl included weathering on the exterior, which resulted from the natural resting position of the bowl. Fire clouding was also present on the exterior.

Portions of a second reconstructible vessel were found near the decorated bowl (Figure 3.2). It was a Mimbres Black-on-white Style I bowl with a rim diameter of 18 cm. Unlike the other vessels recovered from the site, this was a whiteware (white paste); INAA data indicate that it was made in the West Fork of the Gila River to the north of the site. The design consists of a large cross-hatched pattern with some of the border lines embellished with drop pendants. The exterior was highly smoothed.

Two partially reconstructible decorated bowls and a decorated jar were found in Pithouse 22. One bowl was a heavily eroded Mimbres Black-on-white Style 1 vessel found in the trash fill. Portions of the vessel base and parts of one side were found. The second vessel was a Mimbres

Black-on-white Style I/II bowl found in the roof fall/wall fall. About half of the vessel was recovered. It appears from the recovered portion that the vessel was large, with an estimated rim diameter of 24 cm and a depth of at least 15 cm. The painted design showed various areas of oxidation in which the paint appeared as varying shades of red. The vessel was well-made, and the exterior was smoothed but not slipped or polished. Weathering was present on the exterior. Little wear was noted on the rim, but striations were present on the interior. The high overall amount of decoration and use wear suggest its use as a serving bowl or perhaps for food preparation that did not require a heat source as the degree of weathering observed on this bowl is not usually found on serving vessels (Rice 1987).

A third decorated vessel from Pithouse 22 was a Three Circle Red-on-white jar recovered from the floor fill. The smoothed exterior surface of the jar had a scroll design that was heavily eroded and exhibited a large area of fire-clouding. The interior was smoothed and burnished, with minimal evidence of scraping, most likely from manufacture. Although about only about 20 percent of the vessel was present, it appears that this vessel was used for liquid serving given the lack of visible interior use wear and the small size.

One Mimbres Black-on-white Style I bowl was found in the floor fill along the north wall of Pithouse 25 and was apparently stored along the wall (Figure 3.3). The bowl was small, measuring 8.5 cm in diameter and 2.8 cm deep. The design, a hachured spiral, was poorly executed. The exterior was unslipped and dimpled. No visible use wear was noted. This vessel is inferred to represent a novice potter, likely a child.

Plainware and Corrugated Vessels

Eleven complete or partial plainware and corrugated vessels were recovered from La Gila Encantada, 1 plainware bowl and 10 plainware or corrugated jars. No whole or partially reconstructible red ware vessels were found. The vessels were analyzed by Danielle Romero with the goal of providing information on vessel form, size, and function relating to household activities. The same attributes were used to assess function as those used for the decorated wares.

Pithouse 2

The majority of plainware vessels were recovered from the floor of Pithouse 2. One plainware bowl and three jars were recovered near the hearth and were apparently in use when the house burned. One plainware jar was overturned in

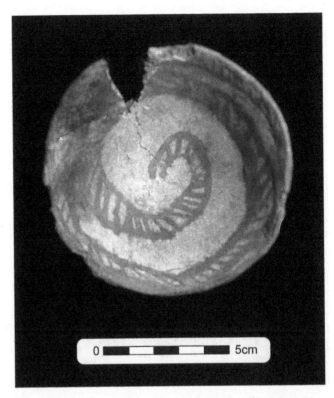

Figure 3.3. Mimbres Black-on-white Style I bowl from the floor of Pithouse 25. Photo by Danielle Romero.

the hearth. It was small (10-cm maximum body diameter; 9.2 cm high) and about 75 percent complete with heavy blackening on both the interior and exterior. This blackening was caused by the house fire and was not the result of use wear. Minor scraping was present on the interior and exterior of the jar, most likely a result of manufacture, and the exterior was not smoothed. The bottom was slightly flattened so the vessel could sit upright. The neck and rim were missing; however, a small fragment of a handle attachment was visible on the body. The vessel was apparently used as a serving vessel and the small size suggests its use for the family living in the house.

Near the hearth was a hemispherical bowl with a rounded rim. It was well-made and nearly complete with a rim diameter of 10.6 cm and a depth of 9.4 cm (Figure 3.4). The burnished exterior had patches of fire-clouding, possibly the result of the vessel being near the fire to heat contents but possibly tied to the house burning. The interior exhibited moderate to heavy scraping with pitting at the very bottom. This bowl had a stable base and an inverted rim indicative of use as a serving vessel for liquid-consistency foods that may have been heated (Hally 1986).

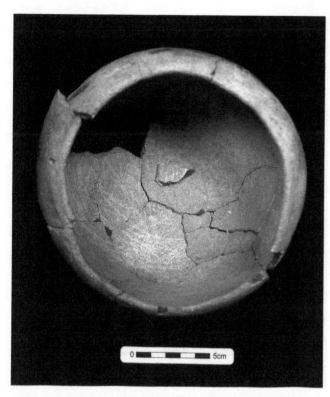

Figure 3.4. Plainware bowl from the floor of Pithouse 2 near the hearth. Photo by Danielle Romero.

Two partially reconstructible jars were also found near the hearth. One was a small (10-cm high) neck-corrugated jar, with about 40 percent of the vessel present. Heavy curvature was noted from the neck and the jar exterior was smoothed but not polished. No interior pitting was noted. The second was the base of a small, neck-corrugated jar that was heavily burned on the exterior, probably from the house fire. It was 30 percent complete; orifice diameter could not be reconstructed but it appears small based on the portions of the rim found.

Pithouse 8

Three jars of Three Circle Neck Corrugated were found in Pithouse 8, two on the floor and one in the roof fall/wall fall. These vessels were all well-made with highly smoothed exteriors. Despite the precision in smoothing, however, the execution of corrugation on the jars was not uniform. The two jars from the pithouse floor both exhibited a high degree of scraping on the upper half of the vessel, while the lower half showed evidence of interior pitting. The scraping on both vessels represented a mixture of striations left during the manufacturing process and from use. The pitting indicates that these jars were most likely used for

storage since no evidence of cooking via burning or blackening was present. The interior pitting on these jars was not heavy and appears to represent liquid storage rather than fermentation, which has been identified by heavy pitting in large jars found at the Harris site (Roth 2015) and NAN Ranch Ruin (Shafer 2012).

One partial Three Circle Neck Corrugated jar was found in the roof fall. It had a rim diameter of 15.5 cm. The exterior of the vessel was burnished with some fire clouding. The interior exhibited heavy use-wear if the form of deep pitting that caused the thickness of the vessel to range from an average of .57 cm to .3 cm in degraded areas. This suggests storage of materials that eroded the base. However, blackening was evident at the shoulder and sooting was present at the base, indicating that the primary use of this jar was for cooking.

Pithouse 22

Three corrugated and plainware jars were recovered from the trash fill of Pithouse 22. The recovery context suggests that the vessels were discarded after they broke. One large Three Circle Neck Corrugated jar rim fragment with a rim diameter of 25 cm was found. This vessel was well made with relatively even coils. The exterior showed signs of fire-clouding and there was some scraping on the interior. The body of the vessel was not recovered, so its function could not be determined; however, a rim diameter of 25 cm suggests a vessel suitable for cooking.

Two plainware jar fragments were found. One had a smoothed exterior and an interior showing signs of scraping, pitting, and light sooting indicative of use as a cooking vessel. The second jar was represented by two very large sections of reconstructed sherds. These sections are assumed to be from the same vessel given similarities in interior use-wear patterns, body thickness, temper, and discoloration and fire-clouding on the exterior. The exterior was smoothed and burnished, and the interior had slight scraping with a large amount of pitting and evidence of sooting near the base. This vessel was most likely a large cooking pot.

Pithouse 25

A small portion of an Alma Plain jar was recovered from the trash fill of Pithouse 25. The exterior was smoothed and burnished. Light pitting, possibly from cooking or storage, was present, along with striations on both surfaces and fire-clouding on the exterior. Like the jar fragments in Pithouse 22, this was most likely discarded in Pithouse 25 after it broke.

Table 3.3. Instrumental Neutron Activation Analysis Results

Feature	Context	Vessel Shape	Pottery Type	INAA Group
Pithouse 2	Roof fall	Bowl	Mimbres Black-on-white Style I	Unassigned
Pithouse 2	Floor	Bowl	Alma Plain	Unassigned
Pithouse 2	Floor	Jar	Alma Plain	Unassigned
Pithouse 2	Floor	Bowl	Mimbres Black-on-white Style I	Unassigned
Pithouse 8	Floor	Bowl	Three Circle red-on-white	Unassigned
Pithouse 8	Floor	Bowl	Mimbres Black-on-white Style I	Gila River
Pithouse 8	Floor	Jar	Three Circle Neck Corrugated	Unassigned
Pithouse 8	Floor	Jar	Three Circle Neck Corrugated	Unassigned
Pithouse 8	Floor	Jar	Three Circle Neck Corrugated	Unassigned
Pithouse 22	Cultural fill	Bowl	Mimbres Black-on-white Style I	Gila River (Woodrow)
Pithouse 22	Roof fall	Jar	Alma Plain	Elk Ridge
Pithouse 22	Floor fill	Jar	Three Circle Red-on-white	Elk Ridge
Pithouse 25	Floor fill	Bowl	Mimbres Black-on-white Style I	Unassigned

Whole Vessel Summary

Only a few households yielded whole or reconstructible decorated, plain, and corrugated vessels. For the most part this matches with the features that had the largest ceramic sherd assemblages. Pithouse 2 provided a unique look at a household assemblage, as the house burned, leaving several vessels in place reflective of daily practices. Overall, the partial and whole vessels recovered from La Gila Encantada represent the range of household forms and uses that would be expected as part of daily domestic activities. The wear across all types fits with the sherd data, which showed that all of the ceramics saw extensive use. The presence of vessels made by young individuals has been noted throughout the Mimbres region and adds further evidence of the value of these vessels outside of a purely functional context.

Instrumental Neutron Activation Analysis (INAA)

Samples from 13 of the decorated, plainware, and corrugated whole and reconstrucible vessels were submitted to the Missouri Research Reactor at the University of Missouri for neutron activation analysis (Table 3.3). This analysis was done as part of a larger project done by Darrell Creel, who was investigating ceramic production in the Mimbres region. Samples from four vessels from Pithouse 2, five from Pithouse 8, three from Pithouse 22, and one from Pithouse 25 were analyzed. The majority (N = 9; 69%) could not be assigned to any known production groups identified in the region (Creel and Speakman 2018). The

two novice-made bowls from Pithouses 2 and 25 could not be assigned, as was the case for all of the other vessels in Pithouse 2, suggesting that the pottery was produced at the site using local clays. The three Three Circle neck corrugated jars and one of the decorated bowls from Pithouse 8 could not be assigned, suggesting local manufacture, while another decorated bowl was from the Gila River Valley. Pithouse 22 had one Mimbres Black-on-white Style I bowl from the Gila River Valley, along with an Alma Plain jar and a Three Circle Red-on-white jar that came from the Elk Ridge production group in the northern portion of the Mimbres River Valley. These data support other site data indicating a focus on local household production throughout the site's occupation.

WORKED SHERDS AND MODELED CLAY ARTIFACTS

Seventy worked sherds and four modeled clay artifacts were recovered from La Gila Encantada; they were analyzed by Linda Gregonis (Gruber and others 2010). The sherds included perforated disks and fragments that were probably used as spindle whorls, unperforated disks and disk fragments with chipped or ground edges, hand-sized pieces that may have served as small dishes, and oblong and trapezoidal shaped pieces. The modeled artifacts included a clay pipe fragment and two possible figurine fragments.

Attributes recorded in the analysis included pottery type or ware, presence or absence of a drilled hole, and metric measurements. The diameters and radii of perforated disks and disk fragments that were thought to be spindle whorls were measured, along with the diameter of the drilled holes. The disks were weighed if they were whole or represented half of an artifact. The purpose of weighing the disks was to determine the weight or type of yarn that may have been spun using the artifact as a spindle whorl. The metric data were compared with information Teague (1998:34–64) has accumulated on spinning technology. For unperforated disks, recorded attributes included edge modification (ground or chipped edges), weathering, decoration, use wear, and special features such as incised or carved lines.

Table 3.4 presents the distribution of worked sherds by feature. Worked sherds were recovered from six pithouse (2,8, 9,14, 22, 25), the midden (Feature 12), and one extramural hearth (Feature 34). For the most part, the worked sherds were found in cultural fill and roof fall/wall fall contexts. More than half of them (N = 37; 53%) came from Pithouse 22. This appears to have more to do with the early age of the house (San Francisco phase) and subsequent use as a trash pit throughout the Three Circle phase rather than a particular characteristic of the resident household.

Perforated Disks and Disk Fragments

Twenty-three perforated disks and disk fragments were found at the La Gila Encantada site. They were recovered in the fill and roof fall/wall fall of several houses (N = 21), as well as in nonfeature contexts (N = 2). Most of the perforated disks were recovered from Pithouse 22 (N = 14). Nineteen of the artifacts were round, one was oval, and three were square with rounded corners. Decorated and undecorated sherds were used to make the disks.

Perforated disks are most often interpreted as spindle whorls, primarily because of their resemblance to ethnographic wood and stone disk whorls. Teague (1998:45-52) has written extensively on ethnographic spindle whorls and archaeological modeled and disk whorls. She found that spindle whorls used to spin fine yarn ranged from about 2 to 4 cm in diameter and from 10 to 22 grams in weight, while those used to spin medium weight yarn ranged from about 4 to 9 cm in diameter and from 26 to 96 grams in weight.

Ten perforated disks (4 half and 6 whole) were weighed in addition to being measured by thickness and diameter (Table 3.5; Figure 3.5). These disks ranged in diameter

Table 3.4. Distribution of Worked Sherds

Artifact Type or Shape	Pottery Type/Ware	0	2	8	9	12	14	22	25	34	Total No. of Artifacts
Perforated Disks, Whole and Fragmentary											
Round	Mimbres Black-on-white Style I					1		1			2
	Indeterminate Mimbres Black-on-white		1					5			6
	Three Circle Red-on-white						1	1			2
	San Francisco Red	1						1			2
	Alma Plain	1					2	4			7
Oval	Alma Plain								1		1
Square	Indeterminate Mimbres Black-on-white						1	1			2
	Alma Plain								1		1
Total Number of Perforated Disks		2	1	0	1	1	3	14	1	0	23
Unperforated Disks, Whole and Fragmentary											
w Ground edges	Indeterminate Mimbres Black-on-white					1		4			5
w Ground edges	San Francisco Red					1					1
w Ground edges	Red or plain							2			2
w Ground edges	Alma Plain		3								3
w Chipped and ground edges	Indeterminate Mimbres Black-on-white							1			1
w Chipped and ground edges	Alma Plain		1				1				2

Table 3.4. (continued)

Artifact Type or Shape	Pottery Type/Ware	Pithouse or Extramural Feature Number									Total No. of Artifacts
		0	2	8	9	12	14	22	25	34	
Unperforated Disks, Whole and Fragmentary (continued)											
w Chipped edges	Mimbres Black-on-white Style I		1								1
w Chipped edges	Three Circle Red-on-white							1			1
w Chipped edges	San Francisco Red	1						1			2
w Chipped edges	Alma Plain						1	2			3
w Incised cross	Indeterminate Mimbres Black-on-white							1			1
w Incised cross	Three Circle Red-on-white							1			1
Five-sided disk	Alma Plain						1				1
Cruciform disk	Redware							1			1
Total Number of Unperforated Disks		1	5	0	2	0	3	14	0	0	25
Dish Forms, Whole and Fragmentary											
Round fragment	San Francisco Red							1			1
Round fragment	Slipped ware								1		1
Round fragment	Alma Plain		1								1
Disk or plate fragment	Alma Plain				1						1
Round or oblong fragment	Indeterminate Mimbres Black-on-white							1			1
Oblong fragment	Indeterminate Mimbres Black-on-white		1					2			3
Oblong or trapezoidal fragment	Indeterminate Mimbres Black-on-white							1			1
Oblong or trapezoidal fragment	Redware						1				1
Trapezoidal fragment	Indeterminate Mimbres Black-on-white							1			1
Trapezoidal fragment	Alma Plain? Slipped	1									1
Total Number of Dish Forms		1	2	1	0	0	1	6	0	1	12
Other Forms, Whole and Fragmentary											
Disk with partial hole	Mimbres Black-on-white Style I				1						1
Circular or oblong disk or dish fragment	Three Circle Red-on-white		1								1
Oblong	Indeterminate Mimbres Black-on-white		2								2
Oblong	Alma Plain	1									1
Oblong	Redware							1			1
Sherd with hole	San Francisco Red						1				1
Square	Indeterminate Mimbres Black-on-white							1			1
Trapezoid	Red ware						1				1
Trapezoid	Indeterminate Mimbres Black-on-white							1			1
Total Number of Other Forms		1	3	1	0	0	2	3	0	0	10
Grand Totals		5	11	2	3	1	9	37	1	1	70

Table 3.5. Perforated Sherd Measurements

Pithouse or Feature Number	Figure 3.5 Letter and FN	Whole or Half	Pottery Type/ Ware	Thickness in millimeters	Diameter in centimeters	Weight in grams	Central hole diameter in millimeters	Number of Artifacts
22	A (FN 452)	half	Mimbres Black-on-white Style I	6	3.7	12	5	1
22	B (FN 92)	half	Alma Plain	6	3.9	12	5	1
22	C (FN 268)	whole	Mimbres Black-on-white	5	4.1 × 4.4	13.8	6	1
0	D (FN 73)	whole	Alma Plain	6	3.8 × 4.2	15	5	1
22	E (FN 268)	whole	Alma Plain	5	4.5	15	5	1
14	F (FN 205)	half	Alma Plain	7	4.2	15.4	7	1
14	G (FN 205)	half	Alma Plain	5	4.6	16.2	10	1
25	H (FN 1181)	whole	Alma plain	6	5 × 5.5	22.3	7 interior	1
22	I (FN 417)	whole	Mimbres Black-on-white	6	5.5	25.8	8	1
22	J (FN 439)	whole	Mimbres Black-on-white	6	5.8 × 6.1	26	8.5	1
							Total no. of Artifacts	**10**

Note: Weights are based on whole artifact; only half and whole measured.

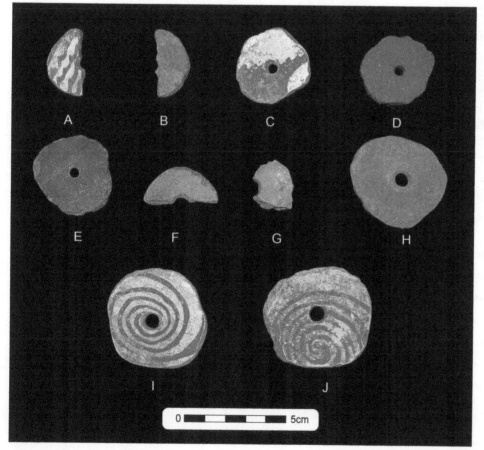

Figure 3.5. Perforated sherd disks: (A) Mimbres Black-on-white Style I from Pithouse 22; (B) Alma Plain from Pithouse 22; (C) Mimbres Black-on-white Style I from Pithouse 22; (D) Alma Plain from general cultural fill; (E) Alma Plain from Pithouse 22; (F) Alma Plain from Pithouse 14; (G) Alma Plain from Pithouse 14; (H) Alma Plain from Pithouse 25; (I) Mimbres Black-on-white Style I from Pithouse 22; and (J) Mimbres Black-on-white Style I from Pithouse 22. Photo by Danielle Romero.

from 3.7 to 5.5 cm and in weight from 12 to 26 grams. As expected, the heaviest sherd disks (Figure 3.5H, I, and J) had the greatest diameters, while the smaller disks were lighter.

Based on the measurement ranges present within the assemblage and using Teague's (1998) size and weight parameters, most of the La Gila Encantada sherds appear to fit a "fine-to-medium-yarn" category. This could include either cotton (for the smaller, lighter disks) and agave or other wild-plant fibers (especially for the heavier disks). Only the largest perforated sherd (6-cm diameter) could be classified as being used to spin medium weight yarn.

Unperforated Disks

Twenty-five unperforated disks and disk fragments were recovered from the site (Table 3.4). They ranged in size

from a small, 1.3-cm-diameter black-on-white piece with ground edges to a 4-cm-diameter Alma Plain disk (Figure 3.6). Over half of the unperforated disks were found in Pithouse 22 including a cruciform disk and two disks with incised crosses.

The cruciform disk was made from a redware sherd. It had well ground edges and what appears to be polish from use. The cross was formed by notching four "corners" to create not-quite equilateral arms (Figure 3.6G). The two sherds with incised crosses were both smaller than the cruciform. One, an indeterminant black-on-white sherd was incised on the exterior and had two notches on either side of one of the cross arms (Figure 3.6C). The other, a Three Circle Red-on-white, was also incised on its exterior, but did not have notches. These distinct pieces, as well as

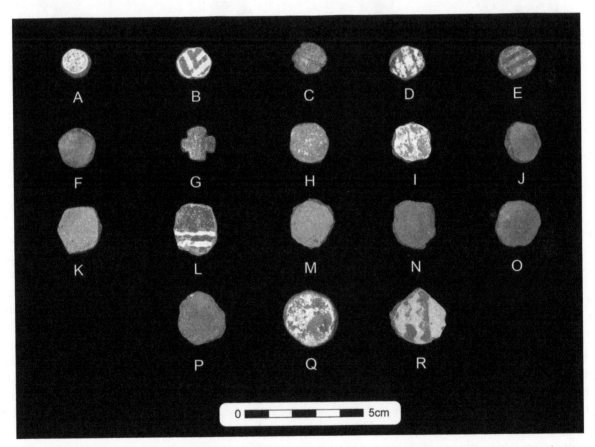

Figure 3.6. Unperforated sherd disks: (A) Mimbres Black-on-white from Pithouse 22; (B) Three Circle Red-on-white from Pithouse 22; (C) Mimbres Black-on-white from Pithouse 22; (D) Mimbres Black-on-white from Pithouse 22; (E) Mimbres Black-on-white from Pithouse 9; (F) Alma Plain from Pithouse 2; (G) unclassified red from Pithouse 22; (H) Alma Plain from Pithouse 2; (I) Three Circle Red-on-white from Pithouse 22; (J) Alma Plain from Pithouse 2; (K) Alma Plain from Pithouse 14; (L) Mimbres Black-on-white Style I from Pithouse 2; (M) Alma Plain from Pithouse 22; (N) Alma Plain from Pithouse 14; (O) Alma Plain from Pithouse 2; (P) Alma Plain from Pithouse 14; (Q) Mimbres Black-on-white from Pithouse 22; and (R) Mimbres Black-on-white from Pithouse 22. Photo by Danielle Romero.

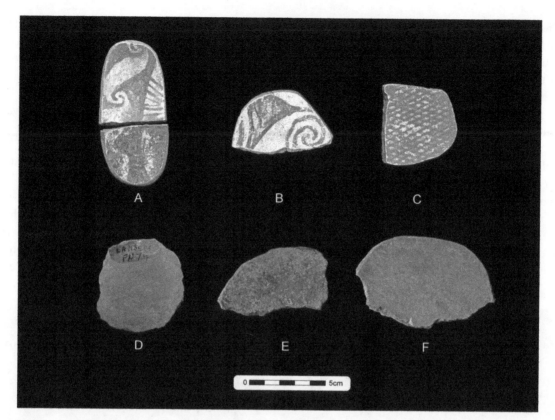

Figure 3.7. Dish forms: (A) Mimbres Black-on-white Style I from Pithouse 2; (B) Mimbres Black-on-white Style I from Pithouse 22; (C) Indeterminate Mimbres Black-on-white from Pithouse 22, floor fill; (D) San Francisco Red from Pithouse 22; (E) slipped brownware from Extramural Feature 34; and (F) Alma Plain from Pithouse 22. Photo by Danielle Romero.

the other small disks from Pithouse 22, may be markers or tokens used in a game much in the same way that wooden markers were used in an O'odham stick game.

Dish Forms

Twelve large sherds with at least one shaped edge were found (Table 3.4; Figure 3.7). They include round, oblong, and trapezoidal shapes that had either ground or chipped edges. They represent an assortment of tools. The round forms have been interpreted as jar covers, while the oblong and trapezoidal shapes have been defined as pottery scrapers, spoons, or scoops (Woosley and McIntyre 1996:197–98).

Pieces from one oblong artifact made from a Mimbres Black-on-white Style I sherd (Figure 3.7A) were found in two different locations in the fill of Pithouse 2 and show different depositional environments, with the largest piece being oxidized to the point where the paint turned brown because it burned in the house fire. This may be a sherd scraper or a gaming piece; similar artifacts have

been found at Hohokam sites and often occur in sets (Gregonis 2006:8.9–8.10). Figure 3.7B and C come from larger artifacts that are more dish-like in shape but neither piece had scraping or scooping use wear, so they were most likely shallow plates. A redware scoop (not pictured) was found in the floor fill of Pithouse 22 and had evidence of heavy wear, with striations on the interior and wear polish on all edges. The remaining dish-like objects (Figure 3.7D, E, F) were round and fall within the jar cover category. Two (Figure 3.7D and F) were found in the fill of Pithouse 22, and the third in Feature 34, an extramural hearth.

Other Forms

Other worked sherds in the collection include oblong and trapezoidal shapes, one Mimbres Black-on-white Style I sherd with a partially drilled hole, and a San Francisco Red sherd with a hole, perhaps part of a set of repair holes. The trapezoidal and oblong pieces have ground edges, and some have polish from wear. The use of pieces like these is not known, but they may have been tokens or markers of some kind.

Modeled Artifacts

Four modeled clay artifacts were found at the site: two possible clay figurines, a clay pipe fragment, and a sherd with a hole that was made when the clay was damp. One of the possible figurines was a log-shaped brownware fragment found in the floor fill of Pithouse 22 and the second was a brownware clay fragment with small indentations on it found in the roof fall/wall fall of Pithouse 22. Figurines, especially broken figurines, are commonly found at larger Pithouse period sites in the Mimbres River Valley; their recovery at La Gila Encantada indicates that their use was widespread.

One clay pipe fragment was found in the fill of Pithouse 22. The interior of the piece was not smoke blackened, so it could be a large bead or part of an effigy, but it resembles other clay pipe fragments recovered from Pithouse period sites in the Mimbres Valley (Haury 1936; Roth 2015). The recovery of a pipe at the site is interesting because they are usually associated with ritual activities in the Mimbres region and no evidence of specialized ritual contexts was found at La Gila Encantada. The fact that the pipe fragment was recovered from trash fill indicates that perhaps some pipes were used in domestic activities, and that the context of smoking was the critical factor in determining the nature of pipe use.

Summary of Worked Sherds

The worked sherds and modeled artifacts recovered from La Gila Encantada include pieces that were probably used as spindle whorls, jar covers, dishes, scoops, scrapers, gaming pieces, and others of uncertain use. The worked sherds were found primarily in trash fill and the roof fall/wall fall of pithouses. Use wear on some of them suggests that they were used repeatedly. Their prevalence at La Gila Encantada indicates that they were commonly used artifacts in domestic activities at the site.

SUMMARY OF CERAMIC DATA

The ceramics recovered from La Gila Encantada provide insights into subsistence practices and household organization. The recovered sherd, whole vessel, and worked sherd assemblage indicate that the bulk of daily domestic activities took place in and around the houses. It appears that cooking and food processing occurred primarily in extramural contexts while serving, storage, and more limited cooking and processing took place within the houses.

These data indicate that daily domestic activities were usually accomplished using undecorated wares, while decorated wares were used primarily for serving. Wear analysis indicates heavy use of the vessels. Worked sherds include small dishes, scrapers, and scoops that were used along with the vessels in food processing. Spindle whorls were prevalent in the trash fill of the houses, indicating that weaving was done at the household level.

Few differences were present among households or through time indicating that the range of domestic activities practiced by these households was the same. No differences in vessel size were observed among households, suggesting similar access to resources, especially storable resources like maize. Few large storage vessels were recovered; this and the low percentage of corrugated sherds may be tied to less intensive agricultural production at La Gila Encantada than what has been found at riverine villages where large storage vessels are present, and corrugated ceramics are more common (Anyon and LeBlanc 1984; Shafer 2003).

The overall small size of the vessels indicates that they were for household use rather than for larger groups. This supports the inference that these households were occupied by families rather than the larger, extended family corporate groups found at the larger riverine villages. The low number of nonlocal ceramics recovered during excavations and the INAA data suggest that these were relatively autonomous households with limited exchange with surrounding groups.

CHAPTER FOUR

Chipped and Ground Stone

Barbara J. Roth, Dylan J. Person, Denise Ruzicka, and Jeffrey R. Ferguson

The goals of the analysis of the chipped and ground stone from La Gila Encantada were to (1) examine activities represented in the tool assemblage to reconstruct household activities; (2) address occupation duration and subsistence strategies; (3) examine lithic technology and determine if changes occurred over time; and (4) reconstruct raw material procurement strategies. Two hundred sixty-one tools, 83 cores, 9,733 pieces of debitage, and 70 ground and pecked stone tools were analyzed for this project. These data provide insights into domestic activities, tool production, and raw material use at the site that address the broader research questions concerning mobility, subsistence strategies, and household organization.

REGIONAL GEOLOGY

The regional geology is important for addressing raw material procurement and use. Locally available materials are predominantly igneous rocks including basalt, andesite, dacite, latite, and large amounts of rhyolite. Sedimentary rocks in the area are associated with Mississippian limestone layers that contain outcrops of chalcedony and chert of various colors (Armstrong 1965). Most of the obsidian found at the site came from sources on Mule Creek, an area west and south of the Mimbres Valley (Ferguson 2010; Shackley 2005). The Mule Creek source area has extensive volcanic deposits that contain numerous obsidian nodules, the smaller of which are colloquially known as "Apache Tears."

For the purposes of the debitage analysis, material types were combined into general categories based on how they were used in the overall La Gila Encantada lithic technological system. The primary categories included rhyolite (rhyolite and andesite combined), basalt, chert, and chalcedony.

CHIPPED STONE TOOLS

The chipped stone tool assemblage from the 2004 and 2005 seasons consisted of 68 projectile points, 79 bifaces, 97 unifaces, 14 core tools, and 3 tabular tools (Table 4.1). Attributes recorded for all tools included tool type, data class (complete, proximal, medial, or distal fragment), platform type (if present), raw material, cortex, and metrics (length, width, thickness for complete tools and size class for broken tools). Additional attributes were recorded for specific tool types. These data were used to examine lithic technology, subsistence practices, and household activities at the site.

Projectile Points

Sixty-eight projectile points and point fragments were recovered at La Gila Encantada. The projectile points were analyzed by Elizabeth Toney and were classified using a typology developed by Dockall (1991) for the Mimbres region, based on his analysis of projectile points from the NAN Ranch Ruin. The projectile point assemblage consisted of 41 arrow and 27 dart points (Table 4.1). These included one Early Archaic stemmed point, 4 Late Archaic San Pedro style dart points, 12 Late Pithouse period dart points (Types D1-D5 in Dockall's classification), 10 dart point fragments, 10 Mimbres arrow points (representing arrow points from the Three Circle phase), 21 other arrow points (Types A1-A4 in Dockall's classification), 5 Classic period arrow points, and 5 projectile point fragments.

Table 4.1. Stone Tool Assemblage

Tool Type	Sub-type	Number	Percentage of Tool Type
Projectile Point			
	Arrow	41	60
	Dart	27	40
Total, projectile points		*68*	*100*
Other Bifaces			
	Drill	9	11
	Knife	9	11
	Preform	7	9
	Ovate	7	9
	Probable projectile point	7	9
	Retouched Flake	3	7
	Scraper	1	(<1)
	Perforator	1	(<1)
	Not assigned	35	44
Total, Other Bifaces		*79*	*100*
Unifaces			
	Retouched flakes	34	35
	Denticulate	26	27
	Notch	6	6
	Scraper	22	23
	Chopper	6	6
	Graver	3	3
Total, Unifaces		*97*	*100*
Core Tools			
	Chopper	7	50
	Denticulate	3	22
	Scraper	2	14
	Core hammerstone	1	7
	Retouched	1	7
Total, Core Tools		*14*	*100*
Tabular Tools		3	
Total Number of Artifacts		**261**	

One lanceolate stemmed point (Figure 4.1), most likely dating to the Early Archaic period, was found on the floor of Pithouse 14, the Georgetown phase structure. It was next to a stone bowl/mortar and a shell bracelet fragment. It is likely a curated piece that has been interpreted as part of the retirement of this house (Roth and Schriever 2015). The other Archaic period points recovered at the site were probably collected and reused by Late Pithouse period groups, as no indication of an earlier Archaic period occupation was found during excavations at the site. It is also possible that an Archaic period occupation was present, but was obliterated by the later Pithouse period occupation.

Most of the points (58%) were found in cultural fill. Seven arrow and two dart points were found in the floor fill of Pithouse 22. As discussed previously, the prevalence

Figure 4.1. Stemmed projectile point from the floor of Pithouse 14, interpreted as part of the ritual retirement of the structure. Photo by Barbara Roth.

of these points is likely because the house was left open for a period of time as it collapsed and was then filled with trash that included at least some of these artifacts. One Mimbres-style arrow point was found in the floor fill of Pithouse 25 and two other points (in addition to the Early Archaic point described previously) were found on the floor in Pithouse 14, including one dart point fragment and a complete obsidian arrow point.

Most of the arrow points (83%) were made of obsidian and all arrow points were made of fine-grained materials (Figure 4.2). Darts were made primarily of chert (44%) and chalcedony (41%). Only one obsidian dart point was found; this may have been a large arrow, but fell within the dart size range.

Roth, Toney, and Lorentzen (2011) used data from La Gila Encantada and the Harris site in the Mimbres River Valley to argue that the bow and arrow was introduced

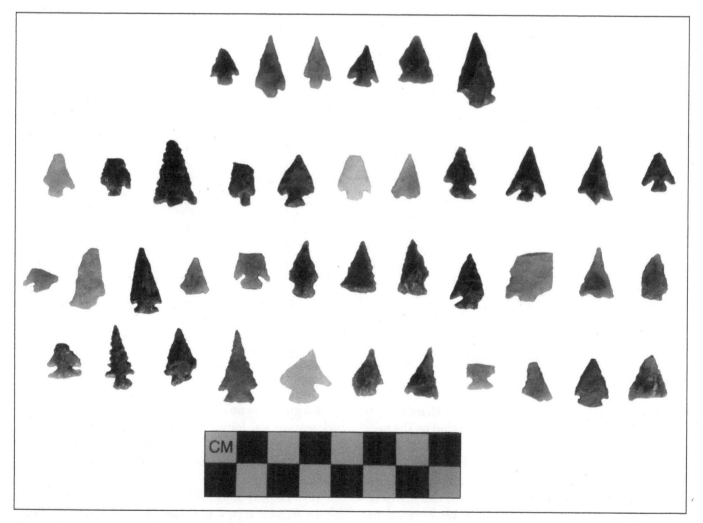

Figure 4.2. Arrow points. Photo by Danielle Romero.

into the Mimbres region during the Georgetown phase, ca A.D. 500. They noted that the use of obsidian increased substantially during the Three Circle phase and tied this to the use of small obsidian nodules for arrow point production. Data from both sites and from others in the Mimbres region point to the continued use of dart points during the Pithouse period.

Other Bifaces

Seventy-nine bifaces were recovered during the excavations at La Gila Encantada. Additional attributes recorded for the bifaces included biface type, stage of reduction, presence of reworking, and fracture type (where applicable). The stage of reduction was determined using a classification system developed by Whittaker (1984) with Stage 1 representing edged blanks, Stage 2 representing preforms, Stage 3 representing refined bifaces, and Stage 4 representing finished bifaces.

For the bifaces that could be assigned to a type, the majority were preforms, drills, and knives (Table 4.1). As expected given the tool types represented, the majority of the bifaces (67%) were Stage 3 or 4; only four were Stage 1.

Most (86%) of the bifaces were broken, which is consistent with their recovery in trash and domestic contexts, as it is likely that they were discarded after use. Although the bifaces were found primarily in the trash fill of pithouses (38%), roof fall also contained a significant number (29%), including drills, knives, and projectile point fragments. Only two biface fragments were found in floor contact, but drills, knives, perforators, a preform, and a projectile point fragment were found in floor fill, documenting their association with household activities. Bifaces were also found in extramural contexts. Preforms were the most common tool type found extramurally; this supports other data indicating that the majority of lithic reduction occurred outside the houses.

Most bifaces were made of chert (41%) or obsidian (27%), followed by fine-grained rhyolite (14%) and chalcedony (11%). This shows a clear preference for the use of fine-grained raw materials and obsidian for biface production. Only two basalt bifaces were found; given the prevalence of basalt in the overall lithic assemblage, it was apparently not a preferred raw material for biface production, perhaps because of the accessibility of other fine-grained raw materials.

Unifaces

The 97 unifaces include a range of tool types that consisted primarily of retouched flakes, denticulates, and scrapers (Table 4.1). Unifaces were relatively evenly distributed in the recovery contexts at the site (36% in cultural fill, 23% in roof fall/wall fall, 26% in floor and floor fill, 15% in extramural areas), but an analysis of tool type by context reveals some interesting patterns. Choppers were found almost exclusively in extramural contexts; only one chopper was found in another context (cultural fill). Choppers, denticulates, and scrapers were the only unifaces found in extramural contexts. The recovery of these tool types in extramural settings indicates that the bulk of food processing activities involving the use of these tool types was done outside the houses. This is supported by edge angle data, which show that tools found in extramural contexts all had steep (over 65 degree) edge angles; steep edge angles are generally inferred to be associated with chopping activities.

Roof fall/wall fall and floor uniface assemblages were similar and included scrapers, denticulates, notches, and retouched flakes. These data support the ground stone data suggesting that roof tops were used as activity areas and show that domestic household activities were performed with these multifunctional tool types.

Most of the unifaces (58%) were complete. All choppers and most denticulates, scrapers, and notches were complete, while retouched flakes were more variable. This suggests that the unifaces were discarded when the edges dulled and were no longer useable rather than when the tool was broken.

Raw materials used for unifaces differ somewhat from those used for bifaces. Rhyolite was the most common raw material (37%) followed by chert (22%), basalt (15%), and obsidian (12%). The only obsidian unifaces were retouched flakes; retouching may have been done both to dull the back of the flake and/or to rejuvenate the edge. Choppers were made of medium- to coarse-grained volcanics, including rhyolite, andesite, and dacite. Denticulates and scrapers were made of rhyolite, chert, or basalt. The prevalence of rhyolite is likely due to both its local abundance and its durability. The prevalence of chert, as with the bifaces, suggests that it was easily accessible.

Core Tools

The 14 core tools consisted primarily of choppers, denticulates, and scrapers (Table 4.1). All the core tools had steep edge angles (over 75 percent) with the exception of the two scrapers. The tools were large, averaging 7 cm in length, and most (64%) weighed over 150 g. They were made primarily of rhyolite (57%) and chert (21%); only one basalt core chopper was found. The recovery context of core tools further reveals the role of roof tops and extramural contexts in processing activities at the site. One battered core chopper/pounding stone was found on the floor of Pithouse 25, but no other core tools were found in the houses.

Tabular Tools

Three tabular tools were found. These are flat pieces of igneous stone with worked edges that are inferred to have been used to remove cactus and agave spines and process fiber. Two complete tools were recovered from cultural fill and one fragment was found in the roof fall/wall fall of Pithouse 14. The complete tools were both made of dacite but the raw material type for the fragment could not be determined. Ethnographically and in the prehistoric Hohokam region tabular tools were associated with agave and fiber processing (Fish and others 1985); it is likely that they were used for similar purposes at La Gila Encantada.

Summary

The chipped stone tool types recovered from La Gila Encantada point to a range of domestic activities and appear to have been specifically geared toward processing activities. If we assume that stone tools found in rooftop assemblages and extramural contexts represent outdoor activities, then the distribution of tools indicates that many of these activities took place outdoors, while manufacturing activities were more likely to have been conducted within the houses.

CORES

The goal of the core and debitage analysis was to address the technology used in stone tool production at La Gila Encantada and to examine raw material procurement strategies. Eighty-three cores were recovered during excavations at the site. Attributes recorded for the cores included raw material, core type, number of flake removals, and weight.

The core data echo the tool data in that rhyolite (39%) and chert (34%) dominated the raw material assemblage. Of the 28 chert cores recovered, 16 (57%) were a green chert that appears to have been obtained locally. The rhyolite graded from a medium- to coarse-grained, locally available form (64% of rhyolite) to a fine-grained form. Basalt accounted for 11 percent of the recovered assemblage, and all the other raw material types (andesite, dacite, quartzite, jasper) accounted for less than 1 percent of the assemblage each. No obsidian cores were found; this is likely because obsidian was procured as small nodules that were shattered

using bipolar technology, so the remaining material was categorized as a tool, flake, or debris.

Where type could be determined, 40 percent of the cores were exhausted (no further removals could be made), indicating heavy use of the raw material. Bifacially reduced cores were also prevalent (22%). In general, the exhausted and bifacial cores were made of the higher quality, fine-grained materials in the assemblage. Basalt was also found predominantly in the form of exhausted or bifacial cores, suggesting that basalt may not have been as readily available or accessible as the local geology would indicate. The single jasper core was exhausted, and it is likely that this material was transported to the site.

Cores were recovered from all contexts at the site but were found primarily in cultural fill (34%) or extramural contexts (28%). The range of recovered core types was also greatest in fill and extramural contexts. These data indicate that core reduction occurred primarily outside of the houses. Some cores were recovered from roof fall/wall fall and house floor contexts and it is likely that these represent cores stored for later use. As discussed in Chapter 2, it is also possible that the cores found in roof fall were components of roof top (and therefore extramural) work areas, or they were used in wall construction. Two burned houses, Pithouses 2 and 8, each had cores on their floors, suggesting that the cores were stored within the houses.

DEBITAGE

The goal of the debitage analysis was to examine lithic reduction strategies and raw material use at La Gila Encantada. Previous work in the Mimbres region has largely focused on the role of debitage as an indicator of decreasing residential mobility and associated changes in subsistence systems. While this approach has provided insights into functional changes related to an increasing reliance on agriculture, it has not investigated the role that debitage played in Mimbres Mogollon lithic technological systems, particularly at outlying Mimbres sites like La Gila Encantada.

Debitage from household contexts was analyzed completely; these included roof fall, floor fill, floor, excavated floor features such as hearths and postholes, and extramural features. Debitage from the remaining strata (trash fill in houses and general extramural contexts) was sampled using a 20 percent random sample. The debitage was analyzed by Dylan Person and Denise Ruzicka.

Debitage was divided into four categories: complete flakes (possessing margins, a platform, and intact termination), proximal flakes (intact margins and platform but lacking intact termination), flake fragments (intact margins but no platform or termination) and debris or shatter (Sullivan and Rozen 1985). For complete and proximal flakes, the type of platform (plain, crushed, faceted, cortical, and absent/other), presence of splitting or lipping, and platform preparation (scarring, trimming, grinding, none, and N/A for absent platforms) were recorded. Cortex percent was recorded for complete flakes and cortex presence/absence was noted for the other categories. Raw material was recorded for all categories. Size measurements (length, width, thickness, and weight) were taken for all complete flakes with digital calipers. Proximal flakes, flake fragments, and debris were assigned a size class ranging from 0.1 to 5 cm after being passed through a series of graduated screens. No artifact was large enough to fail to pass through the 50-mm (5-cm) screen, so this size category was omitted from the analysis results.

Debitage Analysis Results

Nine thousand seven hundred thirty-three pieces of debitage were analyzed from excavated contexts, including debitage collected during the additional excavations of Pithouse 8 in 2009. Table 4.2 presents data on the debitage assemblage. Nearly half of the assemblage (47%) consisted of debris; this is likely due to both the fracture properties of the raw materials and the fact that hard hammer core reduction was practiced at the site. Complete flakes represented almost a quarter (26%) of the assemblage The high percentage of complete flakes is inferred to be a result of the recovery context of the debitage, which emphasized domestic contexts versus generalized trash fill. It follows that more complete flakes would be found where or near where they were used. Flake fragments comprised 16 percent of the assemblage, with proximal flakes slightly less common at 11 percent.

Platform data for complete flakes indicate that plain (single facet) platforms dominate the assemblage (82%). Faceted platforms account for only 6 percent of the

Table 4.2. Artifact Counts by Debitage Category

Artifact Type	Number	Percent
Complete flake	2484	26
Proximal flake	1035	11
Flake fragment	1594	16
Debris/shatter	4620	47
Total Number of Artifacts	**9733**	**100**

Table 4.3. Complete Flake Platform Types

Platform Type	Count	Percentage
Plain	2035	82
Faceted	143	6
Cortical	276	11
Crushed/Absent	30	1
Total Number of Complete Flakes	**2484**	**100**

assemblage, and cortical platforms represent 11 percent (Table 4.3). Most of the crushed platforms (68%) were on obsidian and chert; the brittle nature of these materials makes them higher quality tool stone but they are also more susceptible to breakage when heavy forces are applied during knapping. Only a small percentage of the platforms were lipped (6%) and platform preparation was not common. The low percentage of lipping and platform preparation indicates that, although soft-hammer percussion and tool production and repair were practiced at the site, hard-hammer percussion dominated. This is supported by the high percentage of debris.

Flake terminations can also provide information on flintknapping techniques (Andrefsky 2005; Whittaker 1994). The complete flakes primarily have hinge (65%) and feather (33%) terminations. The feathered flakes are mostly rectangular and blocky rather than thin and tapered, supporting other flake data indicative of the highly expedient and utilitarian nature of the debitage assemblage.

Despite the emphasis on hard-hammer percussion indicated by the flake and platform data, cortex was rare in the overall assemblage. Cortex was measured by the percentage of coverage of complete flakes and by its presence or absence for noncomplete flake categories. Complete flakes largely lack cortex (69%) and flakes with between 1- to 50-percent cortex total 24 percent of the assemblage. Only 7 percent of the complete flakes have more than 50 percent cortex. Data from the complete flakes are supported by data from broken flake and debris, as 78 percent of these lack any cortex. These data suggest that initial cortex removal may have been done at the raw material procurement site and cores were then transported to the site. The low percentage of cortex may also be related to nodule size. Rhyolite, latite, quartzite, and some basalts occur in large nodules and once the cortex was removed, large amounts of usable material would still be available for flintknapping.

Table 4.4. Debitage Raw Material Types

Material Type	Number of Pieces	Percentage
Basalt	1859	19
Chert (Chert/Chalcedony)	3085	32
Latite	171	1.5
Obsidian	354	3.5
Quartzite	66	<1
Rhyolite*	4146	43
Other	52	<1
Total Number of Pieces	**9733**	**100**

*Category includes rhyolite, andesite, and dacite.

Flake size is variable; the average length is 2.5 cm with a range from 0.54 to 8.9 cm and many of the complete flakes are thick and blocky. Weight also varies, with an average of 4.7 g and a range of 0.02–77.5 g. Rhyolite, latite, and quartzite debitage are large and heavy, while chert pieces tend to be smaller. The small size of the chert debitage may be due to its use in tool production and the result of tool repair.

Rhyolite (43%), chert/chalcedony (32%), and basalt (19%) dominate the raw material categories (Table 4.4). These totals reflect the regional geology and support the inference derived from the tool analysis that chert was relatively abundant and accessible. The prevalence of rhyolite in the debitage assemblage is likely a result of its local abundance and flintknapping strategies, as rhyolite occurs predominantly as debris. Chert, too, is primarily represented by debris, although flake fragments are also common. Latite, obsidian, and quartzite represent from 1 to 5 percent of the debitage. With the exception of obsidian, these materials were also locally available, so their low percentage in the assemblage suggests a clear preference for rhyolite and chert in lithic reduction. The low percentage of obsidian debitage is related to the use of bipolar technology and the focus on projectile point manufacture.

Context Data

Although much of the critical context data for debitage in the excavated pithouses (floor, floor fill, roof fall/wall fall) followed the site-level patterning, some variation was present among pithouse contexts. Pithouses 14 and 22, which date earlier in time, had higher proportions of obsidian debitage in floor contexts than later houses, except for Three Circle phase Pithouse 20. Pithouse 14 also had a larger number of obsidian sources than the other houses (Ferguson 2010). This is most likely related

to the higher levels of residential mobility inferred for the earlier occupations that enabled groups to procure obsidian more readily during their seasonal movements. Chert distribution varied during the Three Circle phase, with Pithouses 2 and 25 containing a larger percentage of chert debitage in floor contexts than other houses. This could be the result of storage within the houses given the fact that these two houses represent the only Three Circle phase houses that were not cleaned out completely before they were abandoned.

SUMMARY OF CORE AND DEBITAGE ASSEMBLAGES

The analysis of cores and debitage from La Gila Encantada reveal a highly expedient core and flake reduction system with an emphasis on hard-hammer core reduction and the use of locally available raw materials. The site-level distribution of debitage indicates a very high degree of site-wide homogeneity across both chronological and spatial site contexts.

Raw material use focused on locally available nodules of rhyolite, basalt, and chert. The percentages remained relatively consistent through time, with a slight reduction in the use of obsidian observed in the debitage assemblage. Flake morphology shows that direct, hard-hammer percussion was practiced on cores that had little preparation and were used expediently and opportunistically as they were worked down through the reduction process. The core data show that these local materials were heavily used. Complete flakes were generally rectangular and blocky and showed little evidence of retouch or other types of reuse or modification.

The predominance of hard-hammer percussion suggests that many of the activities conducted at the site were done using sharp flakes that were discarded once their use as a cutting tool diminished. Because of the nature of the raw material and the difficulty in assessing utilized edges, utilized flakes were not recorded during debitage analysis, but many of the flakes, especially the larger ones, have some degree of wear. The distribution of cores and debitage indicates that core reduction took place outside the houses, while some tool repair occurred in the houses.

The La Gila Encantada debitage assemblage fits several expectations derived from lithic studies. Although high quality lithic materials were present throughout the occupation of the site, coarser-grained local raw materials were found more often in Three Circle phase contexts, suggesting a shift in focus to the procurement of locally available stone. This correlates with evidence for increased residential sedentism at La Gila Encantada and fits with

Table 4.5. Obsidian Source Assignment by Phase and Context

Source	Phase				Total Number
	Georgetown	San Francisco	Three Circle	Mixed	
Antelope Wells				1	1
Cow Canyon				2	2
Superior				1	1
Mule Creek-Antelope Creek	22	11	11	375	419
Mule Creek-Mule Mtns	4	4	7	179	194
Mule Creek-Sawmill Creek				11	11
Gwynn Canyon	1		1	15	17
Red Hill				1	1
Unassigned	1		1	3	5
Unassigned-c				2	2
Unassigned-d	1			2	3
Total Number	**29**	**15**	**20**	**592**	**656**

Source: Ferguson 2010.

existing theories regarding raw material use changes between mobile and sedentary groups (Parry and Kelly 1987). Obsidian use decreased and rhyolite replaced chert as a primarily toolstone in some contexts. Because Three Circle phase occupants were apparently spending more time on-site, the assemblage evidence conforms with Andrefsky's (1994) observation that lower quality material use increased when sites were not in immediate proximity to higher quality stone sources. This appears to have been the case at La Gila Encantada.

Despite fitting these models, the overall debitage assemblage did not change through time. It is difficult to determine if this was the result of intentional conservatism on the part of the La Gila Encantada occupants or it represents a broader lithic technological practice present in the Mimbres region.

OBSIDIAN SOURCING

All obsidian artifacts (N = 656) recovered from the site were sourced by Jeffrey Ferguson (2010) of the University of Missouri Research Reactor Archaeometry Laboratory. Compositional analysis was done using X-ray fluorescence. The resulting chemical compositions were compared to known sources in the U.S. Southwest and surrounding regions. X-ray fluorescence was done using a Bruker XRF handheld portable unit. Details on the interpretation of the compositional data are provided in Ferguson (2010).

Most of the obsidian artifacts (95%; N = 624) came from the Mule Creek area, but other sources in Arizona and western New Mexico were also present (Table 4.5). As noted previously, the Mule Creek source area is an extensive volcanic flow that contains numerous obsidian nodules. It has been subdivided into subsources, including Mule Mountains, Antelope Creek, and North Sawmill Creek (Shackley 2005). The subsources are very similar in composition, so in keeping with other recent studies of obsidian sourcing in the Mimbres region (e.g., Taliaferro, Schriever, and Shackley 2010; Roth, DiBenedetto, and Ferguson 2019), they are referred to collectively as the Mule Creek sources for this project.

Source Use by Context

One of the main goals of the obsidian sourcing was to examine source use differences among the three occupation phases at the site to determine if changes in obsidian procurement occurred over time. Only artifacts from floor or floor fill contexts from dated pithouse structures were assigned to a particular phase. Because the vast majority (over 90%) of the obsidian was recovered from cultural fill contexts, there were only between 15 and 29 samples for each of the three phases, making it difficult to attribute too much meaning to subtle differences observed between them. All but 2 of the 61 assigned samples from dated contexts were from the Mule Creek source area, and both were from Gwynn Canyon, a source near Mule Creek.

Table 4.6. Breakdown of Obsidian Source Assignment by Artifact Type

Source	Artifact Type						Total Number
	Unworked	Debitage	Uniface	Core	Biface	Projectile Point	
Antelope Wells		1					1
Cow Canyon		2					2
Superior		1					1
Mule Creek-Antelope Creek		358	8	14	15	24	419
Mule Creek-Mule Mtns	1	159		14	10	10	194
Mule Creek-Sawmill Creek		10			1		11
Gwynn Canyon		11			2	4	17
Red Hill		1					1
Unassigned		5					5
Unassigned - c	1	1					2
Unassigned - d		3					3
Total Numbers	**2**	**552**	**8**	**28**	**28**	**38**	**656**

Source: Ferguson 2010.

Factoring in the small sample sizes, no obvious patterning was present in the distribution of sources by artifact type (Table 4.6). Projectile points exhibited the greatest source diversity, a fact also noted at the Harris site (Roth, DiBenedetto, and Ferguson 2019), but still almost 90 percent were from the Mule Creek source area. The presence of several different sources in the projectile point assemblage may, however, indicate that points were exchanged among Late Pithouse period hunters more often than other obsidian materials, a pattern noted by Roth, DiBenedetto, and Ferguson (2019). Overall, there was little evidence for differences in obsidian procurement and use by phase or artifact type, suggesting a temporally stable pattern of obsidian procurement dominated by material from Mule Creek.

GROUND STONE

The goals of the ground stone analysis were to examine subsistence strategies via a reconstruction of grinding technology and to determine if changes in ground stone technology occurred over time. Attributes recorded for the ground stone assemblage followed Adams (2002) and included artifact type, condition, shape, design, use, processing type (if available), material type, and metric measurements.

Table 4.7 presents data on the 70 ground and pecked stone artifacts and 11 polishing stones recovered from La Gila Encantada by context. As can be seen from the table,

the metates and netherstones represent the largest component of the ground stone assemblage (46%), followed by manos (24%). A small but significant number of mortars and pestles were recovered, indicating that this technology was an important component of subsistence practices at the site and may be associated with walnut, piñon, or possibly cattail processing.

Metates and Netherstones

Eighteen metates and 14 netherstones were recovered from La Gila Encantada (Table 4.7). Netherstones are "bottom stones against which something was worked" and are more expediently made than metates (Adams 2002:143). All but two of the metates were broken, including one that was reused as the base of extramural hearth Feature 39. Three of them were intentionally broken. The metates were made of a range of medium- to coarse-grained materials, including granite and granodiorite, limestone, sandstone, rhyolite, and vesicular basalt. Netherstones were used primarily for manufacturing as they were pecked and, if ground, only lightly ground. One netherstone found on the floor along the east wall of Pithouse 14 had small holes across the surface that may indicate its use for either weaving or as a fire-starter. In contrast to the metates, 57 percent (N = 8) of the netherstones were complete and none were intentionally broken.

The majority of the metates and netherstones were found in roof fall/wall fall contexts, indicating that they

Table 4.7. Ground Stone Artifacts by Context

Artifact Type	Context					Total Number of Artifacts
	Cultural Fill	Roof fall/ Wall fall	Floor fill	Floor	Extramural	
Metate	4	4	4	4	2*	18
Netherstone	2	6	2	4	0	14
Mano	4	5	2	5	1	17
Hammerstone	1	2	1	1	2	7
Mortar	1	3	0	2	0	6
Pestle	0	1	0	1	0	2
Stone bowl	0	0	1	1	0	2
Palette	0	0	0	0	1	1
Polishing stone	2	5	0	1	3	11
Ground stone fragment	1	0	0	0	1	2
Total Number of Artifacts	15	26	10	19	10	80

*includes one metate recovered from Feature 30, secondary occupation of Pithouse 22.

were either used on roof-top work surfaces or may have been stored there. Other than the broken metate found in extramural Feature 39 and a lightly used slab metate found in Feature 30, no metates or netherstones were found in extramural contexts. In contrast, manos were found in both household and extramural contexts. This suggests that metates were not left out, but were instead stored after use.

Metates and netherstones were found in all pithouses excavated at the site, although Pithouse 25 only had one netherstone in the cultural fill. Five metates were found in Pithouse 22; one in cultural fill, one in roof fall/wall fall, one associated with the secondary occupation of the house (Feature 30), and two on the floor. One of the metates on the floor of Pithouse 22 was intentionally broken and covered with red ochre; a second intentionally broken metate was found in the roof fall/wall fall of this house. Roth and Schriever (2015) have interpreted these as part of the ritual retirement of the structure. No netherstones were recovered from Pithouse 22, a surprising fact given the amount of trash deposition present in the house.

One broken, burned metate was found on the floor of Pithouse 2. It was apparently stored along the south wall of the house next to the entryway when the house burned. No manos were found associated with it, but a mano was recovered near an extramural hearth outside the entryway. This house had a surprisingly low amount of ground stone given that it burned while in use.

Pithouse 8 also had a flat-concave metate stored along the wall next to the entryway. The metate had heavy wear

and a triangular-shaped distal end that may have served as a mano rest (Figure 4.3). A compatible mano was found on the floor on the opposite side of the entryway. The mano had been shaped with handholds on the top for a left-handed grinder and the grinding direction on the metate indicates use by a left-handed person. Two metate fragments were found in the floor fill of Pithouse 8. Both were ovoid in shape and exhibited heavy wear. One was

Figure 4.3. Metate and compatible mano from the floor of Pithouse 8. The metate was leaning on the wall north of the entryway and the mano was stacked with a second one along the wall south of the entryway. Photo by Barbara Roth.

initially used for food processing, but the presence of red pigment indicates that it was last used to grind pigment.

A broken metate was found in the floor fill of Pithouse 14, along with five netherstones, three of which were lying on the floor along the east wall of the house. These were apparently stored there and left in place when the house was abandoned. A complete netherstone found on the floor of Pithouse 9 also likely was left there when the house was abandoned.

Manos

Seventeen manos were recovered from La Gila Encantada (Table 4.7). All but one of the manos (from Pithouse 8) were strategically designed, with evidence of pecking and grinding used to shape them. Manos were made on a limited range of raw materials, primarily vesicular basalt and granite.

Like metates and netherstones, manos were recovered from all pithouses. As noted previously, Pithouse 2 had a metate stored along the wall near the entryway, but no mano was found with it. Instead, a complete two-hand trough mano was found outside the house in association with an extramural hearth (Feature 37). A complete mano/pounding stone and a netherstone found in the roof fall/wall fall of Pithouse 2 were likely associated with the roof top work area.

Two manos were found stacked along the wall of Pithouse 8 south of where the metate was found. One was a heavily worn mano that was compatible with the metate previously discussed that had been shaped with handholds made for a left-handed grinder. The second was a granodiorite flat mano with little wear; it does not exhibit any modifications for holding, but this may be because it was just starting to be used.

A large, completely reconstructible (represented by three pieces), two-hand trough mano was found in the roof fall/wall fall of Pithouse 20. It was associated with several other pieces of ground stone, perhaps indicative of a roof-top assemblage. This was the most intensively used of all manos at the site.

Three complete one-hand manos were found on the floor near the hearth of Pithouse 25. Based on the mano characteristics, it appears that one was used for food processing and two were used for both food processing and manufacturing. All three exhibited heavy use wear. One of the multipurpose manos had traces of red ochre on one end, where pecking was present. These manos were found in association with a mortar, pecking stone, and several stone tools.

Mortars

Six mortars were recovered, two of which were reused metates. Two of the mortars were complete. One of the four broken ones, recovered from the floor of Pithouse 8, was intentionally broken and then covered with red ochre. The mortars were recovered from specific contexts; two were found on pithouse floors (Pithouses 8 and 25) and three were in roof fall/wall fall (Pithouses 8, 14, and 20). None of the mortars showed evidence of heavy wear. No residue analysis was done so it is not clear what they were used for; it is possible that they were used for grinding nuts (e.g., walnuts and piñon).

Pestles

Two pestles were found at the site. One was associated with the intentionally broken mortar found on the floor of Pithouse 8. It was complete, circular in shape, and was made of rhyolite. It was worn primarily on one side and exhibited evidence of pecking on the other side that appears to have been done to create hand holds. The second pestle was found in the roof fall/wall fall of Pithouse 25. It, too, was a round pestle that was ground on one end and pecked on the other. It exhibited heavy wear, with evidence of both grinding and pecking.

Hammerstones

Seven hammerstones/pecking stones were recovered. Two were found in extramural contexts and appear to have been used for lithic manufacture, which supports other site data indicating that the bulk of lithic manufacturing took place outside houses.

Two hammerstones were found in Pithouse 22. These appear to have been used for different activities than lithic manufacture. One was found in the roof fall/wall fall of the house and was a complete, circular hammer/pecking stone that had light pecking on all but one end. The second was a hammer/pecking stone found on the floor of the house near the ash pit. It was not shaped but was battered on two ends and appears to have been used for manufacturing or processing activities rather than lithic production.

One hematite pecking stone was found on the floor of Pithouse 25. It was pecked on all sides and there are smoothed areas that appear to be places where the tool was held. Pecking was heaviest on one end, while the other end had some evidence of smoothing, perhaps indicating it was used for different tasks.

Perforated Stone

One perforated stone ("donut stone") fragment was found in the roof fall/wall fall of Pithouse 14. It was made of granodiorite and shows evidence of heavy grinding on both faces and grinding within the hole. The edges were ground, smoothed, and heavily worn. It is not clear what it was used for, but it exhibits evidence of heavy use.

Stone Bowls

One nearly complete stone bowl/mortar and one stone bowl fragment were found in Pithouse 14. The stone bowl fragment was intentionally broken and was found in the floor fill of the house. It was made of granite and was pecked and lightly ground, with a smoothed exterior. The other one was a nearly complete vesicular basalt bowl/mortar found on the floor of Pithouse 14. As noted earlier, it appears that this was placed on the floor intentionally when the house was abandoned and burned. It was circular in shape and ground on the interior, with a smoothed rim. A pollen sample from the bowl yielded corn pollen; it may have been filled with corn as part of the house closure ritual or it may have been used previously to process corn.

Palette

One half of a ground stone palette was found on the extramural work surface in Unit 22 outside Pithouse 2 (Figure 4.4). The palette was heavily ground, and the end was smoothed, perhaps by wear. The two sides were incised with evenly spaced lines. Palettes are commonly recovered in the Hohokam region to the west, where they are thought to have been associated with cremation rituals. They are also present throughout the Late Pithouse period in the Mimbres region but are recovered from both domestic and ritual contexts, indicating that their use varied from the Hohokam. The recovery of a palette fragment in an extramural household context at La Gila Encantada indicates that this was likely a functional item rather than a specialized ritual one.

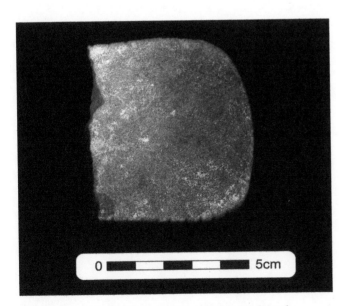

Figure 4.4. Palette fragment from extramural work surface in Unit 22. Photo by Danielle Romero.

Polishing Stones

Eleven polishing stones were recovered from the site and support the inference of on-site household-level ceramic production. All but two were complete and exhibited moderate wear in the form of striations or facets. Most (82%) of the polishing stones were made of fine-grained quartzite, suggesting a clear preference for this material given its rarity in the stone tool assemblage from the site.

The polishing stones were generally found in trash fill, roof fall/wall fall, or extramural contexts. Two of the polishing stones in roof fall/wall fall from Pithouse 2 and one from Pithouse 20 were apparently associated with roof top assemblages. One polishing stone was stored on the floor of Pithouse 8 near the two stacked manos. The recovery contexts suggest that pottery production occurred in extramural contexts.

Miscellaneous Stone Objects

Two stone concretions were found on pithouse floors. One was found on the floor of Pithouse 22. It was a perfect circle, 2.4 cm in diameter, and may have been collected by the house occupants. The second was a sandstone concretion broken in half and placed on the floor of Pithouse 8. Similar concretions have been found in pithouses at Galaz (Anyon and LeBlanc 1984). It is not known if they represent dedicatory behaviors or were simply collected as curiosities by pithouse occupants.

Summary

The ground stone assemblage from La Gila Encantada consists of metates, manos, mortars, and pestles that were used for food processing, pigment and clay grinding, and other manufacturing activities; hammerstones used for lithic production, pecking, and pounding; and polishing stones used in pottery production. The food processing artifacts exhibit heavy wear, and many are multipurpose or reused tools. All but one of the recovered metates was broken. The tool types and wear on the ground stone tools point to relatively intensive food processing activities at the site. The high number of broken metates and mortars on reused metates suggests increasing occupational intensity over time, as most of these were recovered in Three Circle phase contexts (Schlanger 1991). The recovery context of many manos in roof top and extramural contexts indicates that they were used outdoors; however, three complete manos were found around the hearth in Pithouse 25, suggesting that some processing activities were conducted indoors. No metates were found in extramural contexts; they were apparently stored indoors or on roof tops. The location of polishing stones shows that pottery production was also done outdoors and on roof tops. Some of the metates in roof fall/wall fall contexts may, therefore, have been used to grind clay.

Several pieces of ground stone suggest some form of structure retirement behavior. One intentionally broken metate covered with red ochre was found in the floor fill of Pithouse 22 and an intentionally broken mortar with red ochre was found in the floor fill of Pithouse 8. Although it is possible that the metate was used to grind hematite, the intentional breakage and recovery of a mortar in another house with similar characteristics indicates that ground stone may have been ritually "killed" and covered with red ochre when a house was abandoned. Finally, a stone bowl/mortar was placed on the floor of Pithouse 14 before it was burned. The fact that Pithouse 25, which contained a partially depleted but still usable assemblage, and Pithouse 2, which contained a full household assemblage, did not have any killed ground stone or ground stone with red ochre lends support to the idea that intentional breakage and red ochre were part of the decommissioning of Pithouses 8 and 22.

SUMMARY OF CHIPPED AND GROUND STONE

The chipped and ground stone tools recovered from La Gila Encantada contribute to our overall understanding of domestic activities, especially those related to subsistence.

The variety of chipped stone tools recovered illustrate a range of domestic activities, many of which were done with multifunctional tools such as retouched flakes, scrapers, and denticulates. Numerous projectile points were found that support faunal analysis data (Chapter 6), which indicate that deer were commonly hunted by the occupants of La Gila Encantada. The variety of ground stone points to the processing of maize and wild resources, including nuts. The cores and debitage illustrate a highly expedient core and flake reduction strategy. A shift in focus to more locally available raw materials during the Three Circle phase correlates with the decrease in mobility inferred for this phase.

No differences between households were found in terms of the activities performed, lithic reduction strategies, or access to raw materials. These data do, however, point to spatial distinctions in the locations where domestic activities took place. Core reduction was practiced outside, although some raw material was stored inside the houses. Food processing activities were also primarily done outside, as indicated by the recovery of all but one chopper in extramural contexts. Metates were stored inside the houses but the presence of manos and hearths with maize outside of the houses indicates that most of the processing was done outside or perhaps on rooftop activity areas. The distribution of polishing stones indicates that ceramic production was also done in extramural contexts.

CHAPTER FIVE

Shell, Minerals, and Stone and Bone Jewelry

Barbara J. Roth and Arthur W. Vokes

Excavations at La Gila Encantada produced a small assemblage of shell, minerals, and stone jewelry that provide data on personal ornamentation, craft production, exchange relationships, and ritual dedication and retirement practices. Shell and other jewelry are much less common at La Gila Encantada compared to the large assemblages recovered from riverine sites (Anyon and LeBlanc 1984; Roth 2015; Shafer 2003), although sample sizes are not directly comparable. Still, samples from La Gila Encantada were sufficient to recover artifacts with long use lives such as drills and used metates, so it appears that the low numbers of shell and personal ornaments are related to differences in behavior and perhaps access.

SHELL

The 20 pieces of shell recovered during excavations at La Gila Encantada were analyzed by Arthur Vokes (2010), then with the Arizona State Museum. Analysis methods involved creating a written description of each specimen and taking linear measurements. Attributes examined during the analysis included condition, shape, decorative motifs, and technological characteristics. The artifact classification system used in this analysis was based on a system developed by Haury (1937, 1976) for shell recovered from Snaketown in the Hohokam region. The shell nomenclature and biological determinations were made in accordance with Keen's *Sea Shells of Tropical West America* (1971) with additional information obtained from Abbott's *American Seashells* (1974). The terrestrial pelecypods and gastropods were identified using several guides, particularly Abbott's *Compendium of Landshells* (1989).

Table 5.1 presents data on the shell assemblage. Eight whole or partial personal ornaments were found, along with unworked fragments of *Anodonta californiensis*, a freshwater mussel, and *Sonorella* sp., a terrestrial snail. The personal ornaments included four beads and four bracelet fragments, one of which was remodeled. Two of the beads were made of whole *Sonorella* shells (Figure 5.1A). They were were found in the floor fill of Pithouse 25 and likely represent beads from a necklace. *Sonorella* are terrestrial gastropods that are often abundant in upland environments (Bequaert and Miller 1973). The manufacture of beads from these shells is unusual but not unique in southwestern assemblages (Vokes 2010).

The two disk shell beads were recovered together in the floor fill of Pithouse 14 (Figure 5.1B). They may have been part of the ritual retirement assemblage or may be the remains of a broken necklace that was either lost or left when the house was abandoned. Both beads are very similar in size and shape indicating they were likely part of a single strand of beads.

The bracelets included three fragments of plain bracelets (Figure 5.1C–E) and one plain bracelet that had been remodeled (Figure 5.1F). The bracelets were made of *Glycymeris gigantea* from the Gulf of California, the only species of marine shell that was identified during this analysis. Shell bracelets are commonly found at Pithouse period sites in the Mimbres region and are usually interpreted as trade items obtained as finished products from the Hohokam to the west. It is likely that two of the bracelet fragments, one from the floor of Pithouse 14 (Figure 5.1C) and one from the floor fill of Pithouse 25 (Figure 5.1D) represent household dedicatory activities as documented by Roth and Schriever

Table 5.1. Shell Material Summarized by Context

Feature	Context	Artifact Form	Species	Count	MNI	%
Pithouse 2						
	Trash Fill	Unworked fragment	*Anodonta californiensis*	1	?	10%
	Roof Fall/Wall Fall	Unworked fragment	*Anodonta californiensis*	2	?	15%
	Floor Fill	Unworked fragment	*Anodonta californiensis*	1	?	5%
	Floor Fill	Unworked fragment	*Sonorella* sp.	1	1	45%
	Floor	Unworked fragment	*Anodonta californiensis*	1	1	20%
Pithouse 8						
	Trash fill	Reworked bracelet	*Glycymeris gigantea*	1	1	100%
	Floor	Unworked fragment	*Anodonta californiensis*	5	1	15%
	Floor pit fill	Unworked fragment	*Anodonta californiensis*	1	0	5%
Pithouse 14						
	Floor fill/floor	Disk bead	Unidentified marine shell	2	2	100%
	Floor fill/floor	Plain bracelet	*Glycymeris gigantea*	1	1	20%
Pithouse 22						
	Roof fall	Plain bracelet	*Glycymeris gigantea*	1	1	15%
Pithouse 25						
	Floor fill	Whole shell bead	*Sonorella* sp.	2	2	100%
	Floor fill	Plain bracelet	*Glycymeris gigantea*	1	1	15%
Totals				**20**	**11**	

Source: Vokes 2010.
Key:
Count = Total number of fragments present in the sample.
MNI = Estimated number of objects represented in sample.
% = Percentage of artifact represented by recovered piece.

(2015). The bracelet fragment that was found on the floor of Pithouse 14 is interpreted as part of the ritual retirement of this structure (see Chapter 2).

Fragments of *Anodonta californiensis* shell were recovered from Three Circle phase Pithouses 2 and 8. *A. californiensis* is a species of freshwater mussel that would have been available in the Mimbres River (Bequeart and Miller 1973). The mussels may also have been present in Little Walnut Creek, which is directly below the site. It may have been exploited as a local dietary supplement; it is thought to have been consumed by prehistoric populations in the Salt-Gila Basin (Haury 1976:308; Howard 1987:77; Vokes 1988:373). It is also possible that it was used as raw material for carving, although none of the fragments from La Gila Encantada were worked. The fragments recovered from Pithouse 8 probably represent a single shell, with five of the fragments found together on the floor and a sixth piece recovered in the fill of a floor pit.

The small number and limited diversity of the shell assemblage suggests that the occupants of La Gila Encantada were not heavily involved in shell exchange networks. One of the four bracelet fragments was remodeled after it broke, so it appears that marine shell was a valued resource and as such was not easily discarded. Furthermore, the presence of beads fashioned from locally available *Sonorella* shells indicates that the occupants of La Gila Encantada were constrained in their access to nonlocal shell and more dependent on local shell like *Sonorella* and *Anodonta* for raw material to supply the local demand.

MINERALS

Minerals recovered from pithouse contexts have been important in establishing dedicatory and retirement behaviors during the Pithouse period. Minerals such as chrysocolla, quartz crystals, fossils, and mica were

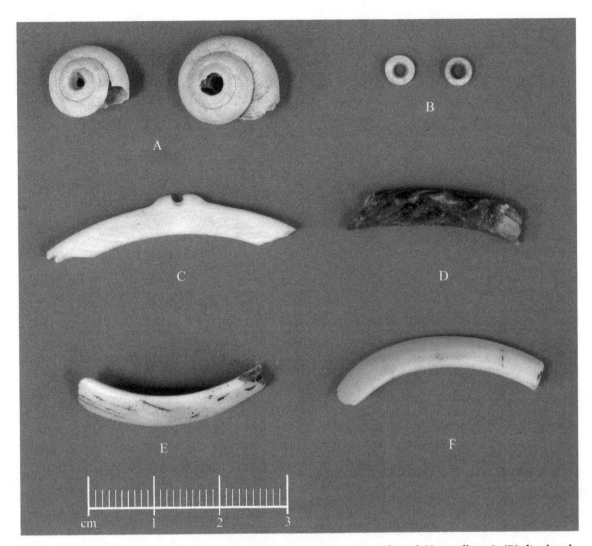

Figure 5.1. Shell artifacts: (A) whole shell beads, perforated terrestrial snail (*Sonorella* sp.); (B) disc beads from the floor fill of Pithouse 14; (C) bracelet fragment from the floor fill of Pithouse 14; (D) bracelet fragment from the floor fill of Pithouse 25; (E) bracelet fragment from the roof fall/wall fall of Pithouse 22; and (F) reworked bracelet fragment from the fill of Pithouse 8. Photo by Arthur W. Vokes.

embedded in the architectural fabric of roofs and walls during construction and placed in postholes prior to the placement of the posts. The presence of these materials in roof fall/wall fall and floor contexts at pithouse period sites in the Mimbres region has been interpreted as representing dedicatory behaviors (Roth and Schriever 2015).

Table 5.2 lists the minerals recovered at La Gila Encantada and their contexts. Chrysocolla was the most common material and was found primarily in roof fall/wall fall and floor contexts. Chrysocolla is a copper-bearing mineral that resembles turquoise and is found in areas where copper deposits are present, so its prevalence at La Gila Encantada is not surprising given the common presence of copper

deposits in the local area. Turquoise and mica were the next most common materials. Mica was found primarily in floor contexts; numerous pieces were found on the floor of Pithouse 8 (one in a posthole) and one piece was found in the floor fill of Pithouse 2. Quartz crystals were also found in cultural fill, roof fall/wall fall, and floor contexts.

The location of minerals (and broken shell bracelets) in roof fall/wall fall indicate that they were placed into the architectural fabric of pithouses when they were built, a common practice documented ethnographically to ensure the protection of the house and household (Ortiz 1969; Saille 1976). Evidence of dedicatory behavior is best seen in Pithouse 22, which contained two fragments of turquoise,

Table 5.2. Minerals Recovered by Context

Mineral Type	Context					Totals
	Cultural Fill	Roof fall/ Wall fall	Floor Fill	Floor	Extramural	
Copper and Associated Minerals						
Azurite				1		1
Brochantite	1					1
Chrysocolla	5	7	1	3		16
Copper			1			1
Malachite		1				1
Turquoise		4		2		6
Other Minerals						
Calcite		1				1
Feldspar		1			1	2
Galina	1					1
Hematite			2			2
Mica	1	1	1	3		6
Pink quartz	1					1
Quartz crystal	2		2			4
Total	11	15	7	9	1	43

one chunk and several smaller fragments of chrysocolla, a quartz crystal, a piece of worked feldspar, a piece of specular hematite, a square piece of calcite, and a fragment of a *Glycymeris* shell bracelet. The roof fall/wall fall of Pithouse 2 also contained materials that can be interpreted as dedicatory, including three pieces of chrysocolla, a chunk of malachite, and a broken stone pendant. With the exception of Pithouse 8, turquoise was only found in roof fall/wall fall contexts. These two related materials (turquoise and chrysocolla) were the most commonly used dedicatory materials in the domestic structures at La Gila Encantada.

STONE AND BONE JEWELRY

One fragment of a stone pendant was found in the roof fall/wall fall of Pithouse 2 and may have been a dedicatory item. The pendant was polished, but it was not possible to determine the type of stone. It appears to have been a geometric design. One small fragment of a rectangular bone ornament with a drilled hole was recovered from the floor of Pithouse 14, the Georgetown phase structure. It was polished and smoothed and was probably a pendant.

No other evidence of jewelry or personal ornaments was identified at the site. As noted previously, this is substantially different from larger riverine pithouse sites, where jewelry is relatively common in the recovered site assemblages and provides further evidence of the distinctive behavior of the occupants living at La Gila Encantada. The use of personal ornaments at larger riverine sites may have been tied to both the greater access to raw materials for ornament production and to finished ornaments, and to the larger and more complex social networks present at these villages. Social interaction at the larger villages may have both allowed for and necessitated personal ornamentation as markers of inclusion within a particular social group. At sites like La Gila Encantada, the difficulty of accessing raw materials like shell for ornament production may have limited the production of shell jewelry. These groups had access to other materials, however, especially stone and bone that could have been used to manufacture ornaments. The lack of ornaments in the La Gila Encantada assemblage is more likely tied to social factors, primarily the small, autonomous households living at the site, rather than differential access.

CHAPTER SIX

Plant and Animal Remains Including Bone Tools

Barbara J. Roth, Pamela J. McBride, Mollie S. Toll, Bruce G. Phillips, and Kari Schmidt Cates

Subsistence strategies at La Gila Encantada were examined using multiple lines of evidence including the artifact data described in the previous chapters supplemented by the analyses of flotation, pollen, and faunal remains recovered during excavations. This chapter summarizes the flotation, pollen, and faunal data in light of the research questions on the interrelationships between subsistence practices, sedentism, and household organization at La Gila Encantada.

FLOTATION DATA

Flotation samples were collected from hearths, pits, ceramic vessels, and other cultural contexts at the site. Samples were collected from all the houses except Pithouse 20, which did not contain any charred material suitable for flotation analysis. Twenty-one samples were analyzed for archaeobotanical evidence by Pamela McBride and Mollie Toll (2010) of the Museum of New Mexico's Office of Archaeological Studies. Seven additional macrobotanical samples were examined to identify roofing material and tree species used for support posts and roof beams in pithouses.

The samples were processed at the Museum of New Mexico's Office of Archaeological Studies. After flotation, each sample was sorted using a series of nested geological screens and then examined under a microsope. Flotation data are reported as standardized counts of seeds per liter of soil rather than the actual number of seeds recovered. Macrobotanical charcoal samples were treated in the same manner as those from flotation samples except that all fragments from a given sample were identified.

Flotation remains were important in examining the subsistence strategies of households at the site. Table 6.1 provides a summary of the results by excavated pithouse and Table 6.2 presents data on the extramural features. Macrobotanical remains from La Gila Encantada are generally like those found at the large riverine sites and, according to McBride and Toll (2010:128), indicate "a broad, stable subsistence regime that began in the early Pithouse period and extended into the Pueblo period."

Maize (*Zea mays*) was the most common edible taxon recovered. It was identified in 15 out of 21 samples. All the houses except Pithouse 25 (and Pithouse 20, which had no samples) had maize. No cultigens other than maize were found, but the lack of beans and squash is more likely due to preservation issues rather than dietary practices (McBride and Toll 2010). Maize cupules were consistently found in extramural hearths, indicating that much of the food processing at La Gila Encantada occurred outdoors. Beans were likely boiled and are thus much less likely to have been preserved in these contexts.

The second most common plant taxon recovered during the flotation analysis was *Chenopodium* sp., which was found in 13 samples. All the house samples (excepting Pithouse 20) yielded chenopod or amaranth (cheno-am) seeds and parts. This is typical of agricultural assemblages, as *Chenopodium* is a weedy annual that grows well in disturbed soils such as agricultural fields.

A sample from bowl contents found in burned Pithouse 2 contained a piñon nut and cone fragments. Piñon (*Pinus edulis*) cone fragments were also found in the hearth of Pithouse 14, indicating household processing of piñon.

Table 6.1. Flotation Analysis Results from Pithouses

Plant	Pithouse (PH) Number and Feature within										
	PH 2 Bowl	PH 2 Hearth	PH 8 Floor pit	PH 8 Posthole	PH 9 Hearth	PH 14 Floor	PH 22 Hearth	PH 22 Storage Pit	PH 22 Ash Pit	PH 22 Floor	PH 25 Hearth
Pine Family											
Piñon pine (*Pinus edulis*)	X					X		X		X	
Ponderosa pine (*Pinus ponderosa*)		X	X	X	X	X	X	X	X	X	X
Pine (*Pinus* sp.)	X					X		X			
Cyprus Family											
Juniper (*Juniperus* sp.)			X		X	X	X	X			X
Grass Family	X		X					X	X		
Maize (*Zea mays*)	X		X	X	X	X		X	X	X	X
Dropseed (*Sporobolus* sp.)							X				
Reed (*Phragmites* sp.)				X		X					
Asparagus Family											
Banana yucca (*Yucca baccata*)						X					
Unknown Monocot		X			X						
Chenopod and Amaranth Families											
Chenopodium sp.	X			X	X	X	X	X	X	X	X
Amaranth (*Amaranthus* sp.)										X	X
Cheno-am					X		X	X	X	X	X
Carpetweed Family											
Purslane (*Portulaca* sp.)			X	X	X	X		X	X		X
Mustard Family											
Mustard (*Brassica* sp.)										X	
Mallow Family											
Globemallow (*Sphaeralcea* sp.)								X	X		
Cactus Family											
Prickly pear (*Opuntia* sp.)						X					
Mint family							X				
Composite Family					X						
Sunflower (*Helianthus* sp.)					X		X				
Other											
Unidentifiable seed									X		X
Unknown		X	X		X		X		X	X	

Source: Data compiled from McBride and Toll (2010).

Table 6.2. Flotation Analysis Results from Extramural Hearths

Plant	Feature Number						
	29	30ᵃ	34	35	36ᵇ	37	39
Pine Family							
Ponderosa pine *Pinus ponderosa*					X (needle)		
Pinus sp.				X (bark)			
Grass Family			X				
Maize (*Zea mays*)	X		X	X	X	X	
Dropseed (*Sporobolus* sp.)		X		X			
Monocot		X			X		
Chenopod and Amaranth Families							
Chenopodium sp.		X		X			X
Cheno-am		X					
Carpetweed Family							
Purslane (*Portulaca* sp.)						X	
Composite Family (Compositae)	X						
Unknown	X			X			

Source: Data drawn from McBride and Toll (2010).
Key: a. Secondary occupation of Pithouse 22.
b. Secondary occupation of Pithouse 14.

Ethnograpic accounts of piñon processing refer to nuts "gathered in the cone," with the cone later "burned off the nuts near where they were gathererd or after the return home" (Reagan 1928:146–47; see also Murphey 1959:23). No piñon remains were recovered from extramural hearths. Ponderosa pine (*Pinus ponderosa*) remains were needles that may have been the result of burning pine in the interior hearths.

Globemallow (*Sphaeralcea* sp.) was recovered from storage and ash pits in Pithouse 22. Although globemallow fruits are edible and several medicinal uses are attributed to this plant, ethnographic accounts from Taos Pueblo show that globemallow pulp was mixed with mud and used to plaster floors (Dunmire and Tierney 1995:187–88). It is thus possible that the plaster used in pithouse hearths and on the floors and walls was made using this mixture, and this would account for the globemallow in the Pithouse 22 floor features.

Evidence for the use of cacti and succulents was restricted to the recovery of a prickly pear (*Opuntia* sp.) seed fragment and a banana yucca (*Yucca baccata*) seed from the floor of Pithouse 14. This Georgetown phase structure is interpreted as representing a seasonally mobile household, so it is possible that the presence of cactus and piñon was tied to seasonal mobility.

The monocot and grass stems found in the houses may have been used to line storage pits, as tinder, or as roofing material. Common reedgrass (*Phragmites* sp.) was found in the storage pit in Pithouse 8 and was possibly used to line the pit. Its presence on the floor of Pithouse 14 may be because the burned roof of Pithouse 14 fell onto the floor, as common reed has been found as a roof closing material (Judd 1954).

Wood charcoal from the flotation samples was primarily juniper and piñon. Both of these species are common in the local environment. Ponderosa pine was found in Pithouse 8 and 14. It is possible that larger roof beams were procured from higher elevations for these houses. Mountain mahogany (*Cercocarpus ledifolius*) charcoal was present in most of the samples. It was likely used as both a source of slow-burning firewood and possibly for the production of wooden tools (McBride and Toll 2010:122).

POLLEN SAMPLES

Pollen samples were analyzed by Bruce Phillips of Eco-Plan Associates, Inc., to supplement the flotation analysis (Phillips and Roth 2010). Eight pollen samples from pithouse floors were analyzed, four of which were pollen washes recovered from artifacts found on the floors. Pollen extraction was done at the Paleoecology Laboratory at Texas A&M University; the extracts were then analyzed by Bruce Phillips at EcoPlan's facility.

Table 6.3 presents the results of the pollen analysis. In general, the pollen assemblage reflected the site setting in a piñon-juniper (*Pinus-Juniperus*) woodland, with oak (*Quercus* sp.) also prevalent. Maize was the only cultigen identified in the pollen samples and was nearly ubiquitous as it was recovered from pithouses dating to all phases. All pithouse samples except Pithouse 22 had cactus pollen. Architectural data indicate that Pithouse 22 was perhaps a winter-occupied house (see Chapter 2), so seasonality (overwintering) may account for the absence of cacti in those samples. Prickly pear (*Opuntia* sp.) and hedgehog (*Echinocereus* sp.) grains were relatively common (Table 6.3) and cactus pollen was recovered from both samples from Pithouse 2, which were taken from bowls on the floor, suggesting that cactus was processed by the house occupants.

Cattail (*Typha* sp.) pollen was recovered from all pithouses but Pithouse 22. The prevalence of cattail pollen suggests regular use of this highly nutritious resource, which was likely found next to Little Walnut Creek. Ethnographic accounts indicate that cattail pollen was collected in the summer and used like flour. Seeds and rhizomes were also processed and eaten, and flowers and stalks could be eaten raw (Rhode 2002). Cattail also had a variety of non-edible uses, including using the fluffy seeds as bedding or padding, so the prevalence of cattail pollen may also be tied to use for these purposes.

The results of pollen analysis support and add to the flotation data. Pollen samples reveal the ubiquitous use of maize, but also document the use of a variety of wild resources, including piñon, cacti, cattails, and cheno-ams. The prevalence of piñon and oak pollen indicate that the local environment was very similar to that observed today.

FAUNAL ANALYSIS

Faunal remains were recovered from all contexts at the site and provided further insights into the site environment and subsistence strategies. Mammal species present in the site vicinity include rabbits (Leporidae), deer and elk (Cervidae), pronghorn (Antilocapridae), carnivores (Felidae, Canidae, Ursidae, Procyonidae, and Mustelidae), and a variety of rodents, including gophers (Geomyidae), ground squirrels (Sciuridae), kangaroo rats (*Dipodomys* sp.), and mice (*Peromyscus* sp.). Birds are also abundant in this biotic community, and some common species include quail (*Callipepla* sp.), sparrows (*Amphispiza* sp.), wrens (*Campylorhynchus* sp.), ravens (*Corvus* sp.), roadrunner (*Geococcyx* sp.), and mourning doves (*Zenaida macroura*).

The faunal analysis was done by Kari Schmidt Cates, then a graduate student in anthropology at the University of New Mexico (Schmidt 2010). Genus and species identifications were made where possible. Following Grayson (1984), other attributes examined during the analysis included element, side, age, fusion, burning, taphonomic factors, breakage patterns, and other surface modifications. Mammals that could not be classified to genus and species were categorized by size following Shaffer and Baker (1992): small mammals (small rodents), small- to- medium sized mammals (leporids and medium sized rodents), medium-sized mammals (large rodents such as beaver, and carnivores such as coyote and fox), medium- to large-sized mammals (deer, bighorn sheep, and pronghorn), and large-sized mammals (bear, elk, and bison).

Several methods were used to quantify the identifiable and unidentifiable faunal remains. These included the number of identified specimens (NISP), the minimum number of individuals (MNI), and lagomorph and artiodactyl indices. The number of identified specimens (NISP) is the number of bones in an assemblage that can be assigned to a particular taxon. Bones were identified to the lowest possible taxonomic level, and the numbers of identifiable specimens within that taxon were tabulated. NISP is the primary method used to determine the abundance of taxa in a faunal assemblage, although it is affected by taphonomic processes, including breakage, differential preservation, recovery techniques, especially screen size, and butchering and transport activities (Grayson 1984). The minimum number of individuals (MNI) in an assemblage is the number that signifies how many animals in a particular taxon are represented. MNI calculation involves "separating the most abundant element of the species found . . . into right and left components and using the greater number as the unit of calculation" (White 1953:397). These two methods were used together to provide a more comprehensive view of the animals used by occupants of La Gila Encantada.

Because artiodactyls (white tail and mule deer, bighorn sheep, elk, and pronghorn) and lagomorphs (jackrabbits and cottontail rabbits) are economically important and

Table 6.3. Pollen Analysis Results—Grain Counts

Plant	Pithouse (PH) Number and Context					
	PH 2 Bowl	PH 8 Floor	PH 14 Hearth	PH14 Bowl	PH 22 Storage Pit	PH 25 Floor
Pine Family (Pinaceae)						
Ponderosa pine (*Pinus ponderosa*)	7		1	4		2
Piñon pine (*Pinus edulis*)	15	6	3	6	5	6
Cypress Family (Cupressaceae)						
Juniper (*Juniperus*)		5	1	5		10
Cattail Family (Typhaceae)						
Cattail (*Typha* sp.)	1	1	5	2		3
Grass family (Poaceae)	17	20	43	28	3	84
Maize (*Zea mays*)	4	1	1	6	14	
Lily family (Lilaceae)	1	1	1			2
Willow family (Salicaceae)						
Willow (*Salix* sp.)						3
Beech Family (Fagaceae)						
Oak (*Quercus* sp.)	5	2	2	19	3	8
Elm Family (Ulmaceae)						
Hackberry (*Celtis* sp.)	4			8		
Buckwheat Family (Polygonaceae)						
Wild buckwheat (*Polygonum* sp.)		1		1		
Chenopod-Amaranth Families (Cheno-ams)	169	94	69	44	47	139
Cactus Family (Cactaceae)						
Prickly pear (*Opuntia* sp.)		2				
Hedgehog Cactus (*Echinocereus* sp.)	2					
Mustard family (Cruciferae)		1	2	2	1	8
Pea family (Leguminosae)	5	3	4	3	2	4
Spurge Family (Euphorbiaceae)						
Spurge (*Euphorbia* sp.)			2			1
Maple Family (Aceraceae)						
Maple (*Acer* sp.)	3			5		1
Rose Family (Rosaceae)	1			3		2
Mint family (Labiatae)			1			1
Nightshade family (Solanaceae)	1			1		1
Composite Family (Compositae)	35	45	32	23	13	61
Liguliflorae						1

Source: Data compiled from Phillips and Roth (2010).

consistently appear in faunal assemblages throughout the Southwest, understanding their importance relative to one another is significant in evaluating subsistence practices and dietary choices (Bayham and Hatch 1985; Szuter 1991). The artiodactyl index (ratio of artiodactyl remains to the sum of artiodactyl and lagomorph remains) and the lagomorph index (ratio of cottontail remains to the sum of all lagomorph remains) were calculated for the faunal assemblage at La Gila Encantada and the indices were used to assess site function, land use, and resource exploitation.

Results

The faunal remains included a moderate sample (N = 947), of which 418 (44%) were identified to at least class (Table 6.4; Schmidt 2010). In general, the bone preservation was good. A small number of bones exhibited some weathering (N = 12), but most of these were found on the surface or only a few centimeters below surface. No evidence for root-etching, carnivore gnawing, or pathologies was found and only one piece of bone had evidence of rodent gnawing. The most common form of modification observed on the faunal remains was burning (N = 308; 32.5%). Eleven pieces of bone were modified into tools and/or ornaments.

Table 6.5 presents the faunal remains recovered from pithouse contexts at the site. A variety of faunal species were used by pithouse inhabitants, but rabbits (*Lepus* sp, *Sylvilagus* sp) and mule deer (*Odocoileus hemionus*) formed the bulk of the assemblage. Cottontail and jackrabbits represent more than 25 percent of the identified remains, and unidentified small- to medium-sized mammals, which are probably mostly leporids, comprise another 20 percent (Schmidt 2010). Cottontails (*Sylvilagus* sp.) were more abundant relative to jackrabbits (*Lepus* sp.), but the exploitation of both species was apparently important. Schmidt (2010:43) suggests that the prevalence of rabbits may be tied to garden hunting practices.

Artiodactyls (mule deer [*Odocoileus hemionus*] and pronghorn [*Antilocapra americana*]) represent 10 percent of the assemblage, and unidentified medium- to large-sized mammals, which are most likely artiodactyls, comprise another 32 percent, suggesting that artiodactyls were a significant component of the diet. These data are consistent with faunal remains from other pithouse sites in the Mimbres region, with a slightly larger component of artiodactyls that may be related to the environmental setting, which provided access to piñon-juniper woodlands and riparian zones. The area around La Gila Encantada may not have experienced the same artiodactyl depletion that has been observed at riverine sites (Cannon 2000,

2003; Schollmeyer 2018). As noted previously, many of the remains exhibited evidence of burning, which suggests that they were consumed.

Other faunal taxa were apparently exploited but do not appear to have been important components of the diet. Rodents were common in the recovered assemblage, but they are likely over-represented by modern, intrusive remains as very few were burned (Schmidt 2010:142).

A variety of bird species were recovered, including Gambel's quail (*Callipepla gambelii*), common raven (*Corvus corax*), turkey vulture (*Cathartes aura*), and turkey (*Meleagris gallopavo*) (Table 6.4). The turkey remains were found in the trash fill and floor of Pithouse 14 and the roof fall/wall fall of Pithouses 20 and 22 (Table 6.5). Given their context, it appears that they were primarily hunted as a food source. Domesticated turkeys have been found a some of the large Classic Mimbres pueblo sites, but none have been found thus far in pithouse contexts. The recovery of turkey bones on the floor of Pithouse 14 along with two perching bird fragments suggests the possibility that bird elements were included in the ritual retirement of the structure.

A mountain lion (*Felis concolor*) bone was recovered from the roof fall/wall fall level of Pithouse 14. The bone was a complete, right first phalanx. Mountain lion remains are relatively rare at pithouse sites, so it is possible that this represents a bone deposited as part of the ritual retirement of Pithouse 14, although its recovery in roof fall/wall fall versus association with the other materials placed on the floor does not support this.

Lagomorph and Artiodactyl Indicies

Table 6.6 presents the lagomorph and artiodactyl indices calculated for the La Gila Encantada faunal assemblage. The prevalence of lagomorphs and artiodactyls is consistent in the prehistoric faunal record of the southwestern United States, although proportionately they varied depending on site location, site function, and other factors relating to agriculture and sedentism (Szuter and Bayham 1989, 1996). The lagomorph index, the ratio of cottontail remains (NISP) to the sum of all lagomorph remains (NISP), generally decreased as an area was more intensively occupied (Bayham and Hatch 1985; Szuter and Bayham 1989, 1996). Cottontails are usually found in areas with denser vegetative cover where they can hide from predators, while jackrabbits prefer open spaces where they can flee from predators (Szuter and Bayham 1996). As groups occupied an area more intensively, they likely had a greater impact on the environment, thus creating a more favorable habitat

Table 6.4. Faunal Remains from All Contexts

Taxon	Totals			Total Burned		
	NISP	MNI	Percent	No.	Percent	Percent of Taxon
Birds						
Perching birds (Passeriformes)	2	1	0.5	0	0	0
Common raven (*Corvus corax*)	3	1	0.7	0	0	0
Gambel's quail (*Callipepla gambelii*)	1	1	0.2	0	0	0
Turkey (*Meleagris gallopavo*)	11	1	2.6	0	0	0
Turkey vulture (*Cathartes aura*)	1	1	0.2	0	0	0
Mammals						
Rodents (Rodentia)	1	1	0.2	0	0	0
Kangaroo rat (*Dipodomys* sp.)	1	1	0.2	0	0	0
Woodrat (*Neotoma* sp.)	18	3	4.3	1	0.6	5.5
Pocket gopher (*Geomys* sp.)	6	3	1.4	0	0	0
Rabbits and hares (Leporidae)	1	1	0.2	0	0	0
Jackrabbit (*Lepus* sp.)	34	3	8.1	11	6.3	32.4
Black-tailed jackrabbit (*Lepus californicus*)	1	1	0.2	0	0	0
Cottontail rabbit (*Sylvilagus* sp.)	57	5	13.8	13	7.5	22.8
Mountain lion (*Felis concolor*)	2	1	0.5	1	0.6	50.0
Artiodactyls (Artiodactyla)	1	1	0.2	0	0	0
Mule deer (*Odocoileus hemionus*)	42	2	10.0	12	6.9	28.6
Pronghorn (*Antilocapra americana*)	1	1	0.2	0	0	0
Small mammal	6	--	1.4	3	1.7	--
Small-medium mammal	84	--	20.2	52	29.8	--
Medium mammal	12	--	2.9	1	0.6	--
Medium-large mammal	133	--	32.0	80	46.0	--
Identified Total (44%)	*418*	--	*100.0*	*174*	*100.0*	--
Unidentified Total (56%)	*529*	--	--	*134*	--	--
Site Totals	**947**	--	--	**308**	--	--

Data compiled from Schmidt 2010.
MNI counts were derived using the mandible.

for jackrabbits than cottontails. The relatively high lagomorph index (0.61) at La Gila Encantada suggests that the exploitation of cottontails was relatively extensive, perhaps reflecting effortless access to these animals.

The artiodactyl index is the ratio of artiodactyl remains divided by the sum of artiodactyl and lagomorph remains (derived from Bayham 1982). Artiodactyl indices throughout the Southwest vary depending on site location. Sites in upland areas typically have indices above 0.30 to 0.35

(Szuter and Bayham 1996). In contrast, lower elevation sites typically have artiodactyl indices below 0.10. The artiodactyl index of 0.32 at La Gila Encantada is consistent with its upland location and suggests that artiodactyl exploitation was important, but perhaps not as important in terms of contributions to total dietary significance when compared to lagomorphs. This may reflect the exploitation of relatively easier to capture small game, perhaps associated with garden hunting.

Table 6.5. Faunal Remains from Pithouse Contexts

Animal	Pithouse (PH) Number							Total NISP
	PH 2	PH 8	PH 9	PH 14	PH 20	PH 22	PH 25	
Birds								
Perching birds				2				2
Common raven			3					3
Gambel's quail				1				1
Turkey				2	5	4		11
Turkey vulture			1					1
Mammals								
Rodents						1		1
Kangaroo rat			1					1
Woodrat	1	1	1	1		12	2	18
Pocket Gopher				4		2		6
Rabbits and hares				1				1
Jackrabbit	3	2		14	3	9	3	34
Black-tailed Jackrabbit		1						1
Cottontail	2	4	4	17	1	24	5	57
Mountain lion			1*	1				2
Artiodactyls						1		1
Mule deer	2	3	1*	18	2		5	31
Pronghorn					1			1
Small Mammal					2	31	2	35
Small-Medium Mammal	11		4	25	7	27	1	75
Medium Mammal	10			2				12
Medium-Large Mammal	20	4	12	65	8	32	14	155
Unidentified	107	1	14	248	16	67	33	486

Source: Data compiled from Schmidt 2010.
Key: *Recovered from disturbed fill.

Table 6.6. Lagomorph and Artiodactyl Indices

Number of Cottontails	Number of all Lagomorphs	Number of Artiodactyls	Lagomorph Index	Artiodactyl Index
57	93	44	0.61	0.32

The species identified in the faunal assemblage from La Gila Encantada suggest that households were exploiting game from a variety of habitats, with a focus on species in woodland habitats including cottontail rabbits, deer, and turkey. These data suggest a focus on local faunal resources, probably due to the prevalence of these animals in the area.

Bone Tools

Eleven bone tools were recovered during excavations at La Gila Encantada; they were analyzed by Courtney Causey. The tools included six awls, two awl/perforators, one spatulate tip, and two worked fragments. Six of the bone tools were recovered together in the roof fall/wall fall of Pithouse 8 (one was in the floor fill but was associated with the group). They were likely stored in the roof rafters, possibly in a perishable container like a hide bag. The tools appear to be part of a kit for basket weaving. They included three complete bone awls, two of which were made from mule deer (*Odocoileus hemionus*) metatarsals. One awl fragment and two perforator/awl fragments were recovered and were likely still in use at the time the pithouse was abandoned. All exhibit relatively heavy wear of the tips and likely broke during use, but were still usable.

One complete concave-tip awl was found in the cultural fill of Pithouse 22. It was from the left tibia of a jackrabbit (*Lepus* sp.) with an intact epiphysis. Little wear was observed on this tool. The four other bone tools from the Pithouses 2 (N =3) and 14 (N =1) are small fragments.

The recovered assemblage is characteristic of bone tools that were primarily used for weaving activities (St-Pierre and Walker 2007). The bone tools from La Gila Encantada do not exhibit the range of tool types and tool sizes found at larger Pithouse period sites.

SUMMARY OF PLANT AND ANIMAL REMAINS

Flotation, pollen, and faunal data from La Gila Encantada reveal a surprisingly stable diet over time in the analyzed samples. Subsistence practices related to plants appear to have focused on cultigens (maize) and wild resources including cacti, cattail, and chenopodium, which were readily available in the site vicinity. The pollen and flotation data point to the importance of cattail, which was probably used as both a food source and for bedding and other nonfood uses. No cultigens other than maize were found, but this is likely due to preservation rather than dietary practices (McBride and Toll 2010). The fact that most of the extramural hearths contained maize cupules suggests that much of the food processing occurred outdoors.

Evidence of maize and piñon nut storage in San Francisco phase Pithouse 22 supports the interpretation of an overwintering strategy, while the presence of maize, piñon nuts, and cacti in burned Three Circle phase Pithouse 2 indicates that the diet was similar through time, with the possible exception of more cacti being used during the Georgetown phase. Other evidence, especially architectural data, point to a reduction in household mobility during the Three Circle phase. Trough manos were found in Three Circle phase contexts, suggesting some increase in agricultural dependence through time, although this is not directly supported by paleobotanical and pollen data. No evidence for changes over time in faunal use are apparent either. The faunal assemblage shows relatively consistent use of rabbits and deer through time.

CHAPTER SEVEN

La Gila Encantada in Regional Context

Archaeological investigations at La Gila Encantada resulted in the complete or partial excavation of seven pithouses and nine associated extramural features dating to all three phases of the Late Pithouse period. These data provide important new insights into the nature of Late Pithouse period occupations at Mimbres Mogollon sites away from the Mimbres River Valley, where much of the previous research on the Late Pithouse period has been conducted (Anyon and LeBlanc 1984; Anyon and Roth 2018; Creel 2006; Creel and Anyon 2003; Roth 2015, 2019b; Shafer 2003; Swanson, Anyon, and Nelson 2012). They show that these nonriverine occupations represent different kinds of adaptations and cultural trajectories than those in the Mimbres (and probably Gila) river valleys.

One of the primary goals of excavations at La Gila Encantada was to explore the variability present in pithouse occupations in the Mimbres region. Research focused on three primary research questions concerning mobility strategies, subsistence practices, and household organization. This chapter examines each of these topics and summarizes the results of investigations at the site in regional context.

La Gila Encantada represents variability in several aspects of occupation when compared to the larger Pithouse period sites in the Mimbres River Valley. It has evidence of seasonal mobility for a longer time span, with sedentism occurring during the Three Circle phase, and less evidence of agricultural intensification than has been proposed for riverine Pithouse period sites (Anyon and Roth 2018; Creel 2006; Roth 2019b; Shafer 2003). Household and community organization appears to have been less complex and ritually focused than at the large riverine pithouse villages (Roth 2019a). The variability represented by La Gila Encantada points to different social situations in these more "rural" non-riverine settings despite sharing overarching similarities in architectural construction methods and ceramic styles that are broadly similar to those in the river valleys, clearly identifying these groups as "Mimbres Mogollon."

MOBILITY STRATEGIES

Data from La Gila Encantada suggest that sedentism increased over time, but groups apparently remained mobile for longer periods than in the Mimbres River Valley. This inference, which is indicated primarily by architectural data, supports interpretations of longer periods of mobility at nonriverine Pithouse period sites suggested by work at the Lake Roberts Vista site in the Sapillo Valley (Roth 2007; Stokes and Roth 1999). At La Gila Encantada, for example, the Georgetown phase house, Pithouse 14, was round, deep, and had an informal hearth consisting of an ash stain on the floor. These architectural traits are generally associated with some level of seasonal mobility (Gilman 1987; Diehl and Gilman 1996). The subsistence data recovered from this house point to the use of a wide range of wild resources and maize, along with hunting of deer and rabbits. These data are consistent with the limited data available on Georgetown subsistence elsewhere in the Mimbres region (Diehl and LeBlanc 2001) and point to broad-scale similarities in the transition to agriculture across this area as groups faced similar challenges in agricultural production.

At the Lake Roberts Vista site, the Georgetown phase component contained a larger variety of obsidian sources and exhibited the use of obsidian from greater distances than the later Pithouse period components (Roth 2007), but this is not the case at La Gila Encantada. At La Gila Encantada, there was no change in obsidian source use from the Georgetown through Three Circle phases and lithic procurement overall was focused on locally available sources (see Chapter 4). This may be because La Gila Encantada is closer to the Mule Creek obsidian source area than the Lake Roberts or Mimbres River Valley sites, making the source more accessible.

The Georgetown phase house (Pithouse 14) at La Gila Encantada was ritually retired (Roth and Schriever 2015). Ritual retirement has been associated with the maintenance of social memory in Neolithic societies in the Near East (Hodder 2007; Hodder and Cessford 2004). It is possible that by the Georgetown phase, the Mimbres people considered this particular spot on the landscape to be important, making the ritual retirement of the house part of commemorative behaviors that linked the occupants to the land. La Gila Encantada is in one of the most productive portions of the Little Walnut Creek Valley, so this behavior may have served as an early form of marking land tenure (Adler 2002). This would suggest that either mobility was decreasing or that groups were marking the site (and probably associated arable land) for their return.

The San Francisco phase component also reflects a certain level of mobility, as Pithouse 22, the excavated San Francisco phase house, represents a winter occupation. The house contained an internal storage pit with abundant maize pollen, indicating the storage of maize. An ash pit found behind the main hearth was most likely a secondary feature used to heat the back of the house. Although the floor assemblage was partially depleted (e.g., no whole vessels were found), the materials found on the floor, which included ground stone, worked sherds, a bone awl, a redware scoop, a hammerstone, and numerous retouched flakes, indicate that a variety of processing and manufacturing activities took place in the house. This would be expected in a winter-occupied house.

The Three Circle phase component at La Gila Encantada represents an increase in sedentism. This again is indicated primarily in the architecture, especially in Pithouse 2, which is rectangular with well-plastered floor, walls, and entryway. Pithouse 25 also contained a well-plastered floor and north wall (the other walls and entryway were not uncovered). Perhaps the best evidence indicating the increase in sedentism during the Three Circle phase comes from the abundance of Three Circle phase trash found in the abandoned pithouses. The Georgetown and San Francisco phase houses were both filled with trash and

contained a wide variety of artifacts, many of which had long use lives (e.g., metates, gaming pieces, and variety of stone tools). In addition, a Three Circle phase secondary occupation was found above the collapsed roof in both houses. As Schlanger (1991) has noted, the presence of artifacts with varying use lives in trash deposits is a key characteristic associated with longer-occupied sites.

Except for the internal storage pit in Pithouse 22, no storage pits were found at La Gila Encantada. This is not unusual for Pithouse period components (Diehl 1997), but Three Circle phase sites in the Mimbres River Valley generally have large storage pits in extramural contexts (Roth 2015). The only extramural features found at La Gila Encantada were hearths and work surfaces. Extramural excavations were generally next to the houses, so it is possible that storage pits were placed farther away from the structures or that storage was done in other types of containers, such as baskets, hide bags, and ceramic vessels. Portions of a number of large jars were found in extramural, roof fall/wall fall, and trash fill contexts; these may have been used for storage.

No burials were found at La Gila Encantada. This is not typical of Pithouse period habitation sites, suggesting a different pattern of occupation than is present at riverine sites. Given the ritual retirement of structures at the site and the architectural and artifact evidence for sedentism by the Three Circle phase, it is surprising that no burials were present. The absence of burials in the trash fill of Pithouse 14 and 22, the earlier houses, is especially unusual, as burials are often found in the fill of pithouses during these periods of occupation. Burials were not placed beneath house floors until the latter part of the Three Circle phase (Shafer 2003). It is possible, but unlikely, that burials were present in other houses at the site. At this time, the lack of burials remains an enigma and something that may be explored with future excavations at other more rural nonriverine sites.

SUBSISTENCE PRACTICES

Subsistence data from La Gila Encantada reveal a broad-spectrum diet encompassing a range of wild resources and maize agriculture. The flotation and pollen samples point to the regular use of maize during all phases of the Pithouse period, as maize was recovered from most of the excavated houses. Maize was the only cultigen recovered at the site, but as McBride and Toll (2010) noted, this may be largely due to preservation issues rather than the lack of squash or beans in the diet. Evidence of the use of a wide range of wild resources, including piñon, chenopodium, amaranth, cattails, sunflower, purslane, globemallow, groundcherry, banana yucca, prickly pear, and hedgehog cactus was found. This broad-spectrum diet was evident in samples from all the excavated houses, indicating that it continued throughout the Pithouse period, although the greatest diversity of plant remains was found in the Georgetown phase structure, possibly indicating that wild resource use decreased over time. Hunting was focused on local fauna including cottontail and jackrabbits and mule deer. This, too, continued throughout the Pithouse period. The subsistence data reflect the abundance of locally available resources and the consistent and continued exploitation of those resources.

The ground stone data suggest that agricultural dependence increased over time. Some observed differences in the ground stone assemblage are likely tied to an increased focus on agriculture. Two trough manos were found during these investigations; both were recovered from Three Circle phase houses. The mano from Three Circle phase Pithouse 20 exhibited the heaviest wear of any of the manos recovered from the site. A broken trough metate was found in the floor fill of Pithouse 20 and a second trough metate fragment was found on the floor of San Francisco phase Pithouse 22. Diehl (1996) has used paleobotanical data to argue that the introduction of a new strain of eight-rowed maize around A.D. 700 led to increased agricultural dependence in the Mogollon region, providing larger yields that were easier to grind than earlier varieties. The new maize variety was apparently correlated with an increase in the use of trough metates, which Adams (1999, 2002) has shown are more efficient for grinding maize. The data from La Gila Encantada reflect this changing technology. It is important to note, however, that despite an increased focus on agricultural production, wild resources remained an important part of the diet during the Three Circle phase and there is no evidence of a shift in dietary preference for cultigens.

HOUSEHOLD ORGANIZATION

Household activities at La Gila Encantada were reconstructed by looking at artifacts and features within houses, in extramural features, and on roof tops. Activities discerned in the artifact assemblages included cooking, food processing, food storage, pottery manufacturing, spinning and weaving, stone tool production, basket manufacturing, and game playing. The location of these activities varied,

with most of the core reduction, pottery production, and food processing taking place outdoors. Most of the flotation samples analyzed from extramural hearths contained maize and most of the choppers and other plant processing tools were recovered from extramural contexts. Cores and hammerstones were also recovered in extramural contexts, although some cores were apparently stored indoors. Debitage from the house floors indicates that some tool repair and perhaps manufacturing also took place indoors.

The distribution of materials on house floors and those associated with extramural features provides information on the location and nature of household activities at La Gila Encantada. Figure 7.1 provides data on the artifact assemblages recovered from floor and floor fill in Pithouses 2, 8, 22, and 25. The bulk of domestic activities took place around pithouse hearths, as indicated by the artifacts found around these features. These artifacts point to a range of household activities, including food processing and preparation, hide working, and other manufacturing activities (woodworking or weaving). The lack of large cooking pots in the ceramic assemblage, even in trash fill and extramural contexts, indicates that food preparation was done primarily for the family and not for larger suprahousehold groups, supporting the inference that the structures represent autonomous households.

The distribution of artifacts within Three Circle phase Pithouse 2, the house that burned accidentally, is very similar to Pithouse 8 (Figure 7.1), but the recovery of a full assemblage provides even more data on household activities in Pithouse 2. Artifacts recovered near the hearth included complete or nearly complete plainware vessels used for cooking and serving, neck-corrugated jars, and several stone tools. A metate was stored along the wall to the west of the entryway. Other materials were found along the west wall of the house and included a decorated bowl that was probably made by a child, chipped stone tools, cores, and several piles of debitage. The cores and debitage are inferred to have been stored for later use.

The back of the house was empty and was probably used as a sleeping area. This inference is supported by the recovery of a large quantity of ash, which may represent burned sleeping mats. The recent recovery of a burned mat fragment on the floor in the back of a Late Pithouse period pithouse at the Elk Ridge site (Roth 2018) indicates that this may have been a common practice valley wide. Few artifacts were found along the east wall to the left of the entryway, in part because this portion of the house did not completely burn, so the occupants probably salvaged

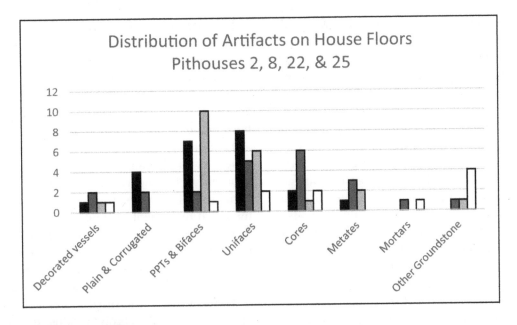

Pithouse 2 ▮
Pithouse 8 ▮
Pithouse 22 ▮
Pithouse 25 ▯

Figure 7.1. Distribution of artifacts on floors of Pithouses 2, 8, 22 and 25. Comparison of decorated, plain, and corrugated vessels, projectile points and bifaces, unifaces, cores, metates, mortars, and other ground stone. Key: PPTs = projectile points.

any artifacts that were present. Several pockets of ash were noted in the floor fill in this portion of the house. These may represent burned perishable materials such as baskets.

No manos were found in the house, but a mano was found associated with a hearth on an extramural surface outside the entryway, suggesting that much of the food processing was done outside. As noted in Chapter 2, Pithouse 2 burned during the summer or early fall when the occupants could spend much of their time outdoors. No rigid gendered division of space was observed in the house (see Roth 2010b). Instead the distribution of artifacts points to flexible use of space around the hearth with evidence of multiple overlapping activities. The exception to this was flintknapping; while cores and piles of debitage were found stored along the wall, it appears that all flintknapping took place outdoors.

The artifacts found in Pithouse 8, which also burned but had a partially depleted assemblage, further support the inferences gleaned from Pithouse 2. Although it dates earlier in the Three Circle phase, the nature of the recovered

materials are remarkably similar to those found in Pithouse 2. Complete or nearly complete ceramic bowls and neck-corrugated jars were found near the hearth. One large metate was found stored along the wall near the entryway.

The differences that are apparent between the households appear to be related to household size and individual occupants. Both bowls from Pithouse 8 were decorated and the sizes of the bowls and jars from Pithouse 8 were larger than those from Pithouse 2. This is potentially tied to family size. Bone tools were recovered from the roof fall of Pithouse 8 and are inferred to have been stored there; none were found in Pithouse 2. The bone artifacts from Pithouse 8 were weaving tools, indicating that at least one of the occupants of Pithouse 8 was a basketweaver, perhaps doing this for intra-site exchange. Pithouse 8 also had a different metate form than was observed anywhere else on the site, a triangular top that was probably used as a mano rest. One unique aspect of this metate is that the woman using it was left-handed. A left-handed mano that had finger grooves and was compatible with the metate was found near it. This is an important reminder that individuals lived in these households (Tringham 1991).

The assemblage from Pithouse 25 was partially depleted; no ceramic vessels were recovered except for a small Mimbres Black-on-white Style I child's bowl found near the north wall. A range of chipped stone tools and ground stone were found in the excavated portion of the house around the hearth, however, including three manos, a metate fragment, a core, chopper, pecking stone, and a denticulate. These tools point to processing and manufacturing activities. They further support the inference that a variety of activities were performed within the houses and that the use of space was flexible and tied to household versus gender-specific domestic activities.

Excavations at La Gila Encantada have also established that flat roof tops were used as extramural work and tool storage areas, at least during the Three Circle phase. Two houses, Pithouses 2 and 20, contained the remains of these roof top work areas, which included ground stone (including polishing stones) and worked sherds. These data suggest that a variety of processing and manufacturing activities took place in these settings. A possible roof top work area, represented by three manos, two hammerstones, several cores, and numerous worked sherds, was found in San Francisco phase Pithouse 22. Unfortunately, because of the way the house decomposed, it is not clear if the artifacts were all associated with the house or represent trash fill. Their location in one excavation unit rather than being distributed throughout the entire house fill suggests that they represent a roof top assemblage. This would indicate that the practice began during the San Francisco phase.

The most significant differences between the occupation of La Gila Encantada and other Pithouse period sites investigated in the region are apparent in overall site organization (Roth 2019a). Data from La Gila Encantada indicate that pithouses and their associated extramural features were used by autonomous households during all phases of the Late Pithouse period. This is supported by the layout of the houses, which was revealed by the magnetometer survey results and mapping of the site. The houses are distributed across the site in discrete areas; no clusters of houses or patterning in regard to orientation was observed, in sharp contrast to the pithouse clusters interpreted as the remains of extended family corporate groups found in the Mimbres River Valley (Creel 2006; Roth 2019b; Roth and Baustian 2015; Shafer 2003).

The artifact assemblages recovered from the houses also point to the presence of relatively autonomous households.

Little evidence of craft specialization is apparent, with the possible exception of weaving indicated by the bone tools in Pithouse 8. Similar artifact types including ceramics, ground stone, and chipped stone tools, were found in all houses. In general, vessel size suggests use for the immediate family versus larger groups, again except for the larger bowl found on the floor of Pithouse 8.

Household ritual appears to have been an important aspect of the lifeways of pithouse occupants. This is apparent in the incorporation of numerous dedicatory items into the architectural fabric of pithouses and in the ritual retirement of houses. Chrysocolla, turquoise, quartz crystals, and shell bracelet fragments were placed into the roofs and walls when houses were built (Roth and Schriever 2015). These same kinds of materials were placed in communal structures in the Mimbres region (Creel and Anyon 2003). The ritual retirement of the pithouses involved placing objects on the house floors prior to abandonment. Pithouse 14 had a stone bowl/mortar, an Early Archaic projectile point, and a shell bracelet fragment that were apparently placed on the floor before the house was burned. Pithouse 22 had an intentionally broken metate covered with red ochre placed on its floor and Pithouse 8 had an intentionally broken mortar covered with red ochre on its floor. This evidence of dedicatory and retirement behaviors documents the significance of household ritual to the occupants of La Gila Encantada.

Despite the emphasis on household ritual, the absence of a great kiva at La Gila Encantada indicates that the residents were not hosting communal rituals. Gilman and Stone (2013) note that great kivas served to provide social relationships with spatially distinct families and settlements, so the occupants of La Gila Encantada most likely went to other nearby sites for community rituals. As with the burials, future research at additional nonriverine sites may shed light on this issue.

The final inference that can be made about households at La Gila Encantada is that they were not participating in region-wide social networks and were, for the most part, self-sufficient. The materials recovered from the houses point to household-level production. Non-Mimbres pottery and shell are rare at the site. The bulk of lithic procurement appears to have been done locally, with some obsidian procurement focused on the Mule Creek sources, which are not far away. It is likely that cooperation occurred during farming, hunting, and gathering forays, but the data from La Gila Encantada do not indicate that households participated regularly in a wider social network. This is further supported by the fact that no communal structures were found at the site. This suggests that groups were traveling elsewhere for community-based gatherings.

SUMMARY

Excavations at La Gila Encantada enhance our understanding of the occupation of the Mimbres region during the Pithouse period by offering glimpses of site use away from the major river valleys. The site was occupied during all phases of the Late Pithouse period and evidence points to increasing sedentism thorough time. The diet was stable through most of the occupation, focusing on maize agriculture supplemented with a variety of wild plants and hunted game. There is some evidence in the recovered ground stone assemblage that agricultural dependence increased during the Three Circle phase. This increased sedentism and agricultural dependence did not have a dramatic effect on household organization, however, as household layout and activities were similar through time, from at least the San Francisco phase on. Ritual activities were part of the construction and decommissioning of houses, and it appears that household ritual was important to the site occupants. The absence of a great kiva indicates that broader communal integrative efforts were either not practiced or took place in other settings, perhaps at larger villages surrounding the site.

These data support Swanson, Anyon, and Nelson's (2012) assessment that many pithouse period occupations were smaller and less formal than the larger pithouse villages found along the Mimbres and Gila rivers. Households at La Gila Encantada were autonomous and self-sufficient. These "rural" populations appear to have been prevalent throughout the area. They likely interacted to some degree with the larger villages and others in the region, as indicated by the small amounts of shell and nonlocal pottery recovered at La Gila Encantada, but they were largely independent from what was going on at the larger villages. As such, they provide another picture of the Pithouse period in the Mimbres region, once less formal and socially complex, but clearly prevalent and likely important in the daily lives of those who lived in the region.

The role that these smaller sites played in the transition to pueblos that occurred in the A.D. 1000s has not been investigated. La Gila Encantada was no longer occupied by the A.D. 900s, so did not participate in this transition, but it is likely that many other smaller pithouse villages were still occupied as the transition occurred. There are many lines of inquiry that remain to be addressed with data from these nonriverine sites.

Appendix

PROJECT PARTICIPANTS

2004 Season

Project Director:	Barbara J. Roth
Field Director:	Leon Lorentzen
Lab Director:	Bernard Schriever
Crew Chiefs:	Jodi Dalton
	Robert Hickerson

Field School Students:	Christoper Brosman
	Rod Campbell
	Dan Gardner
	Mark Ladwig
	Shane Rumsey
	Adam Scerini
	Ryan Schmidt

Volunteers:	Nancy Curtis
	Marilyn Markel
	Carol McCanless
	Regina Mueller
	Sara Shugert
	Steve Swanson
	Judy & Carroll Welch

2005 Season

Project Director:	Barbara J. Roth
Field Director:	Leon Lorentzen
Lab Director:	Bernard Schriever
Crew Chief:	Robert Hickerson

Field School Students:	Ilan Ackerman
	Stephanie Busby
	Zachary Butt
	Christina Dykstra
	Jennifer Edwards
	Misty Fields
	Elisa George
	Libby Kunkler
	William "Lighthawk" Tolbert
	Elizabeth Toney

Volunteers:	Nick Beale
	Nancy Curtis
	Tom Gruber
	Marilyn Markel
	Carol McCanless
	Kyle Meredith
	Josh Reeves
	Sara Shugert
	Matthew Taliaferro
	Judy & Carroll Welch

References Cited

Abbott, R. Tucker
   1974   *American Seashells: The Marine Mollusca of the Atlantic and Pacific Coasts of North America,* 2nd edition. Van Nostrand Reinhold, New York.
   1989   *Compendium of Landshells: A Full-Color Guide to More then 2,000 of the World's Terrestrial Shells.* American Malacologists, Melbourne, Florida.

Adams, Jenny L.
   1999   Refocusing the Role of Food-grinding Tools as Correlates for Subsistence Strategies in the U.S. Southwest. *American Antiquity* 64:475–498.
   2002   *Ground Stone Analysis, A Technological Approach.* University of Utah Press, Salt Lake City.

Adler, Michael
   2002   The Ancestral Pueblo Community as Structure and Strategy. In *Seeking the Center Place: Archaeology and Ancient Communities in the Mesa Verde Region,* edited by Mark Varien and Richard Wilshusen, pp. 25–40. University of Utah Press, Salt Lake City.

Andrefsky, William Jr.
   1994   Raw Material Availability and the Organization of Technology. *American Antiquity* 59:21–34.
   2005   *Lithics: Macroscopic Approaches to Analysis.* Cambridge University Press, New York.

Anyon, Roger
   1980   The Late Pithouse Period. In *An Archaeological Synthesis of South-central and Southwestern New Mexico,* edited by Steven A. LeBlanc and Michael Whalen, pp. 142–204. Office of Contract Archaeology, University of New Mexico, Albuquerque.

Anyon, Roger, and Steven A. LeBlanc
   1980   The Architectural Evolution of Mogollon-Mimbres Communal Structures. *Kiva* 45:253–277.
   1984   *The Galaz Ruin.* Maxwell Museum of Anthropology, Albuquerque.

Anyon, Roger, and Barbara J. Roth
   2018   Changing Perspectives on Pithouse Period Occupations in the Mimbres Region. In *New Perspectives on Mimbres Archaeology, Three Millennia of Human Occupation in the North American Southwest,* edited by Barbara J. Roth, Patricia A. Gilman, and Roger Anyon, pp. 48–63. University of Arizona Press, Tucson.

Anyon, Roger, Patricia A. Gilman, and Steven A. LeBlanc
   1981   A Reevaluation of the Mogollon-Mimbres Archaeological Sequence. *Kiva* 46:209–225.

Anyon, Roger, Darrell Creel, Patricia A. Gilman, Steven A. LeBlanc, Myles R. Miller, Stephen E. Nash, Margaret C. Nelson, Kathryn J. Putsavage, Barbara J. Roth, Karen Gust Schollmeyer, Jakob W. Sedig, and Christopher A. Turnbow
   2017   Re-evaluating the Mimbres Region Prehispanic Chronometric Record. *Kiva* 83:316–343.

Armstrong, A. K.
1965 The Stratigraphy and Facies of the Mississippian Strata of Southwestern New Mexico. In *Guidebook of Southwestern New Mexico II.* New Mexico Geological Society, Sixteenth Field Conference, Socorro.

Bayham, Frank E.
1982 *A Diachronic Analysis of Prehistoric Animal Exploitation at Ventana Cave.* Unpublished Ph.D. dissertation, Department of Anthropology, Arizona State University, Tempe.

Bayham, Frank E., and P. Hatch
1985 Archaeofaunal Remains from the New River Area. In *Hohokam Settlement and Economic System in the Central New River Drainage, Arizona*, edited by David E. Doyel and Mark D. Elson, pp. 405–433. Publication in Archaeology No. 4. Soil Systems, Inc., Phoenix.

Bequaert, Joseph C., and Walter B. Miller
1973 *The Mollusks of the Arid Southwest, with an Arizona Check List.* University of Arizona Press, Tucson.

Blanton, Richard E.
1994 *Houses and Households: A Comparative Study.* Plenum, New York.

Bussey, Stanley D.
1975 *The Archaeology of Lee Village: A Preliminary Report.* COAS Publishing, Las Cruces, New Mexico.

Cannon, Michael D.
2000 Large Mammal Relative Abundance in Pithouse and Pueblo Period Archaeofaunas from Southwestern New Mexico: Resource Depression among the Mimbres Mogollon? *Journal of Anthropological Archaeology* 19:317–347.
2003 A Model of Central Place Forager Prey Choice: An Application to Faunal Remains from the Mimbres Valley, New Mexico. *Journal of Anthropological Archaeology* 22:1–25.

Ciolek-Torrello, Richard
1985 A Typology of Room Function at Grasshopper Pueblo. *Journal of Field Archaeology* 12:41–65.

Cosgrove, Harriet S., and Cornelius B. Cosgrove
1932 *The Swarts Ruin: A Typical Mimbres Site in Southwestern New Mexico.* Papers of the Peabody Museum of American Archaeology and Ethnology 15(1). Harvard University, Cambridge.

Creel, Darrell G.
2006 *Excavations at the Old Town Ruin, Luna County, New Mexico, 1989–2003.* Department of the Interior, US Bureau of Land Management, New Mexico State Office, Santa Fe.

Creel, Darrell G., and Roger Anyon
2003 New Interpretations of Mimbres Public Architecture and Space: Implications for Cultural Change. *American Antiquity* 68:67–92.

Creel, Darrell, and Harry J. Shafer
2015 Mimbres Great Kivas and Plazas during the Three Circle Phase, ca. AD 850–1000. *Kiva* 81:164–178.

Creel, Darrell, and Robert J. Speakman
2018 Mimbres Pottery, New Perspectives on Production and Distribution. In *New Perspectives on Mimbres Archaeology: Three Millennia of Human Occupation in the North American Southwest*, edited by Barbara J. Roth, Patricia A. Gilman, and Roger Anyon, pp. 132–148. University of Arizona Press, Tucson.

Creel, Darrell, Roger Anyon, and Barbara Roth
2015 Ritual Construction, Use, and Retirement of Mimbres Three Circle Phase Great Kivas. *Kiva* 81:201–219.

Crown, Patricia L.
2001 Learning to Make Pottery in the Prehispanic American Southwest. *Journal of Anthropological Research* 57:451–469.
2002 Learning and Teaching in the Prehispanic American Southwest. In *Children in the Prehistoric Puebloan Southwest*, edited by Kathryn A. Kamp, pp. 108–124. University of Utah Press, Salt Lake City.

Diehl, Michael W.
1996 The Intensity of Maize Processing and Production in Upland Mogollon Pithouse Villages, A.D. 200–1000. *American Antiquity* 61:102–115.
1997 Changes in Architecture and Land Use Strategies in the American Southwest: Upland Mogollon Pithouse Dwellers, A.C. 200-1000. *Journal of Field Archaeology* 24:179–194.
1998 The Interpretation of Archaeological Floor Assemblages: A Case Study from the

American Southwest. *American Antiquity* 63:617–634.

2001 Competing Models of Upland Mogollon Pithouse Period Life-Styles. In *Early Pithouse Villages of the Mimbres Valley and Beyond: The McAnally and Thompson Sites in their Cultural and Ecological Contexts,* by Michael W. Diehl and Steven A. LeBlanc, pp. 25–36. Papers of the Peabody Museum of Archaeology and Ethnology Vol. 83, Harvard University, Cambridge.

Diehl, Michael W., and Patricia Gilman
1996 Implications from the Designs of Different Southwestern Architectural Forms. In *Interpreting Southwestern Diversity: Underlying Principles and Overarching Patterns,* edited by Paul R. Fish and J. Jefferson Reid, pp. 189–194. Anthropological Papers No. 48. Arizona State University, Tempe.

Diehl, Michael W., and Steven A. LeBlanc
2001 *Early Pithouse Villages of the Mimbres Valley and Beyond: The McAnally and Thompson Sites in their Cultural and Ecological Contexts.* Papers of the Peabody Museum of Archaeology and Ethnology Vol. 83, Harvard University, Cambridge.

Dockall, John E.
1991 *Chipped Stone Technology at the NAN Ruin, Grant County, New Mexico.* Unpublished M.A. thesis, Department of Anthropology, Texas A&M University, College Station.

Douglass, John G., and Nancy Gonlin (editors)
2012 *Ancient Households of the Americas.* University Press of Colorado, Boulder.

Dunmire, William W., and Gail D. Tierney
1995 *Wild Plants of the Pueblo Province.* Museum of New Mexico Press, Santa Fe.

Ferguson, Jeffrey R.
2010 X-Ray Fluorescence of Obsidian Artifacts from La Gila Encantada (LA113467), New Mexico. Archaeometry Laboratory letter report, Research Reactor Center, University of Missouri, Columbia.

Fish, Suzanne K., Paul R. Fish, Charles Miksicek, and John Madsen
1985 Prehistoric Agave Cultivation in Southern Arizona. *Desert Plants* 7:107–112.

Gilman, Patricia A.
1987 Architecture as Artifact: Pit Structures and Pueblos in the American Southwest. *American Antiquity* 52:538–564.

Gilman, Patricia A., and Tammy Stone
2013 The Role of Ritual Variability in Social Negotiations of Early Communities: Great Kiva Homogeneity and Heterogeneity in the Mogollon Region of the North American Southwest. *American Antiquity* 78:607–623.

Grayson, Donald K.
1984 *Quantitative Zooarchaeology: Topics in the Analysis of Archaeological Faunas.* Academic Press, New York.

Gregonis, Linda M.
2006 Ceramic Analysis. In *The Cultural Resources of Quail Creek: Archaeological Excavations at AZ EE:1:317 (Shell Man), AZ EE:1:275, AZ EE:1:175, AZ EE:1:176, and AZ EE:1:302(ASM),* edited by Michael D. Cook, pp. 8.1–8.44. Cultural Resource Report No. 2006-42. Westland Resources, Inc., Tucson.

Gruber, Thomas, Christina Dykstra, Linda M. Gregonis, and Barbara Roth
2010 Ceramic Analysis. In *Archaeological Investigations at La Gila Encantada* (LA 113467), *Grant County, New Mexico,* pp. 54–87. Report submitted to the Archaeological Conservancy, Albuquerque.

Hally, David J.
1986 The Identification of Vessel Function: A Case Study from Northwest Georgia. *American Antiquity* 51:267–295.

Hard, Robert J.
1990 Agriculture Dependence in the Mountain Mogollon. In *Perspectives on Southwestern Prehistory,* edited by Paul E. Minnis and Charles L. Redman, pp. 135–149. Westview Press, Boulder.

Haury, Emil W.
1936 *The Mogollon Culture of Southwestern New Mexico.* Medallion Papers No. 20. Gila Pueblo, Globe.
1937 Shell. In *Excavations at Snaketown: Material Culture,* by Harold S. Gladwin, Emil W. Haury, E. B. Sayles, and Nora Gladwin,

Haury, Emil W. (continued)
   pp:135–153. Medallion Papers, No. 25. Gila Pueblo, Globe.
1976   *The Hohokam: Desert Farmers & Craftsmen, Excavations at Snaketown, 1964–1965.* University of Arizona Press, Tucson.

Henrickson, Elizabeth F., and Mary M. A. McDonald
1983   Ceramic Form and Function: An Ethnographic Search and An Archaeological Application. *American Anthropologist* 85: 630–643.

Hodder, Ian
2007   Catalhoyuk in the Context of the Middle Eastern Neolithic. *Annual Review of Anthropology* 36:105–120.

Hodder, Ian, and Craig Cessford
2004   Daily Practice and Social Memory at Catalhoyuk. *American Antiquity* 69:17–40.

Howard, Ann Valdo
1987   The La Ciudad Shell Assemblage. In *Specialized Studies in the Economy, Environment and Culture of La Cuidad,* edited by Jo Ann E. Kisselburg, Glen E. Rice, and Brenda L. Shears, 75–174. Office of Cultural Resource Management Anthropological Field Studies, 24(1). Arizona State University, Tempe.

Judd, Neil M.
1954   The Material Culture of Pueblo Bonito. Miscellaneous Collections No. 124. Smithsonian Institution, Washington D.C.

Keeley, Lawrence H.
1988   Hunter-gatherer Economic Complexity and "Population Pressure": A Cross-cultural Analysis. *Journal of Anthropological Archaeology* 7:373–411.

Keen, A. Myra
1971   *Sea Shells of Tropical West America; Marine Mollusks from Baja California to Peru,* 2nd edition. Stanford University Press, Stanford.

Kelly, Robert H.
1992   Mobility/Sedentism: Concepts, Archaeological Measures, and Effects. *Annual Review of Anthropology* 21:43–66.

Kent, Susan
1992   Studying Variability in the Archeological Record: An Ethnoarchaeological Model for Distinguishing Mobility Patterns. *American Antiquity* 57:635–660.

Kramer, Carol
1982   Ethnographic Households and Archaeological Interpretation. *American Behavioral Scientist* 25: 663–675.

Lightfoot, Kent G.
1984   *The Duncan Project: A Study of the Occupation Duration and Settlement Pattern of an Early Mogollon Pithouse Village.* Anthropological Field Studies No. 6. Arizona State University, Tempe.

Lowell, Julia C.
1991   *Prehistoric Households at Turkey Creek Pueblo, Arizona.* Anthropological Papers No. 54. University of Arizona Press, Tucson.

Lucas, Jason
2007   Three Circle Phase Architectural Variability among the Mimbres-Mogollon. In *Exploring Variability in Mogollon Pithouses,* edited by Barbara J. Roth and Robert Stokes, pp. 71–80. Anthropological Research Papers No. 58. Arizona State University, Tempe.

McBride, Pamela J., and Mollie S. Toll
2010   Plant Remains from La Gila Encantada. In *Archaeological Investigations at La Gila Encantada (LA 113467), Grant County, New Mexico,* pp. 114–129. Report submitted to the Archaeological Conservancy, Albuquerque.

Murphey, Edith Van Allen
1959   *Indian Uses of Native Plants.* Mendocino County Historical Society, Fort Bragg, California.

Netting, Robert M., Richard R. Wilk, and Eric J. Arnould
1984   *Households: Comparative and Historical Studies of the Domestic Group.* University of California Press, Berkeley.

Ortiz, Alfonso
1969   *The Tewa World: Space, Time, Being and Becoming in a Pueblo Society.* University of Chicago Press, Chicago.

Parry, William J., and Robert L. Kelly
1987   Expedient Core Technology and Sedentism. In *The Organization of Core Technology,* edited by J. K. Johson, and C.A. Morrow, pp. 285–304. Westview Press, Boulder.

Phillips, Bruce, and Barbara J. Roth
2010 Pollen Analysis. In *Archaeological Investigations at La Gila Encantada (LA 113467), Grant County, New Mexico*, pp. 130–132. Report submitted to the Archaeological Conservancy, Albuquerque.

Rafferty, Janet E.
1985 The Archaeological Record on Sedentariness: Recognition, Development, and Implications. In *Advances in Archaeological Method and Theory* 8:113–153. Academic Press, New York.

Reagan, Albert B.
1928 Plants Used by the White Mountain Apache of Arizona. *The Wisconsin Archeologist* 8:143–161.

Rhode, David
2002 *Native Plants of Southern Nevada, an Ethnobotany.* University of Utah Press, Salt Lake City.

Rice, Glen E.
2003 *A Research Design for the Study of Hohokam Houses and Households.* Technical Report No. 2003-05. P-MIP, Tempe.

Rice, Prudence
1987 *Pottery Analysis: A Sourcebook.* University of Chicago Press, Chicago.

Rogers, Michael, Kevin Faehndrich, Barbara J. Roth, and Greg Shear
2010 Cesium Magnetometer Surveys of a Pithouse Site near Silver City, New Mexico. *Journal of Archaeological Science* 37:1102–1109.

Roth, Barbara J.
2004 Preliminary Archaeological Fieldwork at La Gila Encantada, Southwestern New Mexico. Report submitted to the Archaeological Conservancy, Albuquerque.
2007 The Late Pithouse Period Occupation of the Lake Roberts Vista Site. In *Exploring Variability in Mogollon Pithouses*, edited by Barbara J. Roth and Robert Stokes, pp. 5–11. Anthropological Research Papers No. 58. Arizona State University, Tempe.
2010a *Archaeological Investigations at La Gila Encantada (LA 113467), Grant County, New Mexico.* Report submitted to the Archaeological Conservancy, Albuquerque.
2010b Engendering Mimbres Mogollon Pithouses. In *Engendering Households in the Prehistoric Southwest*, edited by Barbara J. Roth, pp. 136–152. University of Arizona Press, Tucson.
2015 *Archaeological Investigations at the Harris Site, LA 1867, Grant County, Southwestern New Mexico.* Report on file, Department of Anthropology, University of Nevada, Las Vegas.
2018 *Report on 2017 Archaeological Investigations at the Elk Ridge Site (LA 79863), Mimbres Valley, Grant County, New Mexico.* Report submitted to the US Forest Service, Gila National Forest, Silver City.
2019b Pithouse Community Development at the Harris Site, Southwestern New Mexico. In *Communities and Households in the Greater American Southwest*, edited by Robert J. Stokes, pp. 183–200. University Press of Colorado, Louisville.
2019a Identifying Social Units and Social Interaction during the Pithouse Period in the Mimbres Region, Southwestern New Mexico. In *Interaction and Connectivity in the Greater Southwest*, edited by Karen G. Harry and Barbara J. Roth, pp. 133–150. University Press of Colorado, Louisville.

Roth, Barbara J., and Kathryn M. Baustian
2015 Kin Groups and Social Power at the Harris Site, Southwestern New Mexico. *American Antiquity* 80:451–471.

Roth, Barbara J., and Bernard Schriever
2015 Ritual Dedication and Retirement at Mimbres Valley Pithouse Sites. *Kiva* 81:179–200.

Roth, Barbara J., Katelyn DiBenedetto, and Jeffrey R. Ferguson
2019 Obsidian Procurement and Social Interaction at the Harris Site, Mimbres Valley, New Mexico. *Journal of Archaeological Science: Reports* 27:1–9.

Roth, Barbara J., Elizabeth Toney, and Leon Lorentzen
2011 The Advent of Bow and Arrow Technology in the Mimbres Mogollon Region. *Kiva* 77:87–109.

Saille, David G.
1976 Pueblo Building Rituals: Religious Aspects of a Productive Activity. Manuscript on file,

Saille, David G. (continued)
Arizona State Museum Library, University of Arizona, Tucson.

Schlanger, Sarah
1991 On Manos, Metates, and the History of Site Occupations. *American Antiquity* 56:460–474.

Schmidt, Kari M.
2010 Faunal Remains from Excavations at La Gila Encantada. In *Archaeological Investigations at La Gila Encantada (LA 113467), Grant County, New Mexico*, pp. 133–143. Report submitted to the Archaeological Conservancy, Albuquerque.

Schollmeyer, Karen Gust
2018 Long Term Interactions of People and Animals in the Mimbres Region, Southwest New Mexico AD 200–1450. *Kiva* 84:51–84.

Sedig, Jakob W.
2015 *The Mimbres Transitional Phase: Examining Social, Demographic, and Environmental Resilience and Vulnerability from A.D. 900-1000 in Southwest New Mexico.* Unpublished Ph.D. dissertation, Department of Anthropology, University of Colorado, Boulder.

Seymour, Deni
1990 *A Methodological Perspective on the Use and Organization of Space: A Case Study of Hohokam Structures from Snaketown, Arizona.* Unpublished Ph.D. dissertation, Department of Anthropology, University of Arizona, Tucson.

Shackley, M. Steven
2005 *Obsidian: Geology and Archaeology in the North American Southwest.* University of Arizona Press, Tucson.

Shafer, Harry J.
2003 *Mimbres Archaeology at the NAN Ranch Ruin.* University of New Mexico Press, Albuquerque.
2006 Extended Families to Corporate Groups: Pithouse to Pueblo Transformation of Mimbres Society. In *Mimbres Society*, edited by Valli S. Powell-Marti and Patricia A. Gilman, pp. 15–31. University of Arizona Press, Tucson.
2012 Possible Archaeological Evidence for Classic Mimbres Use of Tesquino at the NAN Ranch Ruin, Southwest, New Mexico. In *Collected Papers from the 17th Biennial Mogollon Archaeology Conference*, edited by Lonnie C. Ludeman, pp. 109–118. Privately published by Lonnie Ludeman, Las Cruces.

Shafer, Harry J., and Robbie L. Brewington
1995 Microstylistic Changes in Mimbres Black-on-White Pottery: Examples from the NAN Ruin, Grant County, New Mexico. *Kiva* 61:5–29.

Shaffer, Brian S., and B. W. Baker
1992 *A Vertebrate Faunal Analysis Coding System with North American Taxonomy and dBase Support Programs and Procedures.* Technical Report No. 23. Museum of Anthropology, University of Michigan, Ann Arbor.

Sinopoli, Carla M.
1991 *Approaches to Archaeological Ceramics.* Plenum Press, New York.

St-Pierre, C. Gates, and C. W. Walker (editors)
2007 *Bones as Tools: Current Methods and Interpretations in Worked Bone Studies.* BAR International Series No. 1622. British Archaeological Reports, Oxford.

Sternberg, Robert S.
1982 *Archaeomagnetic Secular Variation of Direction and Paleointensity in the American Southwest.* Unpublished Ph.D. dissertation, Department of Geosciences, University of Arizona, Tucson.

Stokes, Robert J.
1995 *Prehistoric Settlement Patterns in the Sapillo Creek Valley, Gila National Forest, New Mexico.* Unpublished M.A. thesis, Department of Anthropology, Eastern New Mexico University, Portales.

Stokes, Robert J. (editor)
2019 *Communities and Households in the Greater American Southwest.* University Press of Colorado, Boulder.

Stokes, Robert J., and Barbara J. Roth
1999 Mobility, Sedentism, and Settlement Patterns in Transition: The Late Pithouse Period in the Sapillo Valley, New Mexico. *Journal of Field Archaeology* 26:423–434.

Stuiver, M., P.J. Reimer, and T.F. Braziunas
1998 High-precision Radiocarbon Age Calibration for Terrestrial and Marine Samples. *Radiocarbon* 40:1127–1151.

Sullivan, Alan, and Kenneth C. Rozen
1995   Debitage Analysis and Archaeological Interpretation. *American Anthropologist* 50: 755–779.

Swanson, Steve, Roger Anyon, and Margaret C. Nelson
2012   Southern Mogollon Pithouse Period Settlement Dynamics, Land Use, and Community Development, A.D. 200-1000. In *Southwestern Pithouse Communities, A.D. 200–900*, edited by Lisa C. Young and Sarah A. Herr, pp. 95–109. University of Arizona Press, Tucson.

Szuter, Christine R.
1991   *Hunting by Prehistoric Horticulturalists in the American Southwest*. Garland, New York.

Szuter, Christine R., and Frank E. Bayham
1989   Sedentism and Animal Procurement among Desert Horticulturalists of the North American Southwest. In *Farmers as Hunters: The Implications of Sedentism*, edited by Susan Kent, pp. 80–95. Cambridge University Press, Cambridge, England.
1996   Faunal Exploitation During the Late Archaic and Early Ceramic/Pioneer Periods in South-Central Arizona. In *Early Formative Adaptations in the Southern Southwest*, edited by Barbara J. Roth, pp. 65–72. Prehistory Press, Madison, Wisconsin.

Taliaferro, Matthew S., Bernard A. Schriever, and M. Steven Shackley
2010   Obsidian Procurement, Least Cost Path Analysis, and Social Interaction in the Mimbres Area of Southwestern New Mexico. *Journal of Archaeological Science* 37:536–548.

Teague, Lynn S.
1998   *Textiles in Southwestern Prehistory*. University of New Mexico Press, Albuquerque.

Tringham, Ruth
1991   Households with Faces: the Challenge of Gender in Prehistoric Architectural Remains.

In *Engendering Archaeology: Women and Prehistory*, edited by Joan M. Gero and Margaret W. Conkey, pp. 93–131. Blackwell, Oxford.

Vokes, Arthur W.
1988   Shell Artifacts. In *The 1982–1984 Excavations at Las Colinas: Material Culture*, by David R. Abbott, Kim E. Beckwith, Patricia L. Crown, R. Thomas Euler, David A. Gregory, J. Ronald London, Marilyn B. Saul, Larry A. Schwalbe, Mary Bernard-Shaw, Christine R. Szuter, and Arthur W. Vokes, pp. 319–384. Archaeological Series No. 162, Vol. 4. Arizona State Museum, University of Arizona, Tucson.
2010   Shell Artifact Analysis. In *Archaeological Investigations at La Gila Encantada (LA 113467), Grant County, New Mexico*, pp. 144–149. Report submitted to the Archaeological Conservancy, Albuquerque.

Wheat, Joe Ben
1955   *Mogollon Culture prior to A.D. 1000*. Memoirs No. 10. Society for American Archaeology, Washington D.C.

White, Theodore E.
1953   A Method of Calculating the Dietary Percentages of Various Food Animals Utilized by Aboriginal Peoples. *American Antiquity* 18:396–398.

Whittaker, John C.
1994   *Flintknapping: Making and Understanding Stone Tools*. University of Texas Press, Austin.

Wilk, Richard R., and William L. Rathje
1982   Household Archaeology. *American Behavioral Scientist* 25:617-639.

Woosley, Anne I., and Allan J. McIntyre
1996   *Mimbres Mogollon Archaeology: Charles C. DiPeso's Excavations at Wind Mountain*. University of New Mexico Press, Albuquerque.

Index

ABSTRACT

This volume explores variability in Pithouse period (A.D. 550–1000) occupations in the Mimbres Mogollon region of southwestern New Mexico using a case study of the La Gila Enacantada site. Archaeological excavations at the site yielded architectural, artifact, and subsistence data documenting an occupation away from the Mimbres and Gila River valleys that shows different economic and social trajectories than those seen at the larger riverine pithouse villages. The data point to differences in sedentism, subsistence strategies, and household organization in these more "rural" nonriverine settings. La Gila Encantada occupants were mobile for a longer time span and did not intensify their agricultural production. Their household and community organization appears to have been less complex and less ritually focused than that at the larger riverine villages, with autonomous households present throughout the sequence of occupation. These data enhance our understanding of the Pithouse period by documenting site use away from the river valleys, which highlight the dynamic nature of Pithouse period settlements in the region.

RESUMEN

Este volumen explora la variabilidad en las ocupaciones del período Pithouse (550-1000 d. C.) en la región de Mimbres Mogollon del suroeste de Nuevo México utilizando un estudio del sitio de La Gila Enacantada. Las excavaciones arqueológicas en el sitio arrojaron datos arquitectónicos, de artefactos y de subsistencia que documentan una ocupación lejos de los valles de los ríos Mimbres y Gila que muestran trayectorias económicas y sociales diferentes a las que se ven en los pueblos de pozos fluviales más grandes. Los datos apuntan a diferencias en el sedentismo, las estrategias de subsistencia y la organización del hogar en estos entornos no riverinos más "rurales". Los ocupantes de La Gila Encantada fueron móviles durante más tiempo y no intensificaron su producción agrícola. Su organización doméstica y comunitaria parece haber sido menos compleja y menos centrada ritualmente que la de las aldeas fluviales más grandes, con hogares autónomos presentes a lo largo de la secuencia de ocupación. Estos datos mejoran nuestra comprensión del período Pithouse al documentar el uso del sitio lejos de los valles fluviales, lo que pone de relieve la naturaleza dinámica de los asentamientos del período Pithouse en la región.

ANTHROPOLOGICAL PAPERS OF THE UNIVERSITY OF ARIZONA